**ANCHOR BOOKS**

A LIFE OF RHYME

Edited by

James Feeke

First published in Great Britain in 2003 by
ANCHOR BOOKS
Remus House,
Coltsfoot Drive,
Peterborough, PE2 9JX
Telephone (01733) 898102

All Rights Reserved

Copyright Contributors 2003

HB ISBN 1 84418 186 3
SB ISBN 1 84418 187 1

FOREWORD

Anchor Books is a small press, established in 1992, with the aim of promoting readable poetry to as wide an audience as possible.

We hope to establish an outlet for writers of poetry who may have struggled to see their work in print.

The poems presented here have been selected from many entries, and as always editing proved to be a difficult task.

I trust this selection will delight and please the authors and all those who enjoy reading poetry.

James Feeke
Editor

Contents

I Married A Comedian's Nightmare	Paul Kelly	1
Laugh Out Loud	Laura Squibb	2
I'd Rather Not	George Saurombe	3
Angel Walking	George Speechley	4
Imagine	Margaret Suffolk	5
Working Man's Hand/Feet	Gail Sturgess	6
Wearing Out	Kathleen South	7
I Have Loved Thee	Thomas R Slater	8
Unique	Mary Anne Scott	9
Untitled	N A Smith	10
Only You	Victor Shaw	11
Drowning	Nic Scanlan	12
Eine Klein Nacht Musik	Roger Stevens	13
Ravello's Track Record	Robert D Shooter	14
Loneliness	John L Wright	15
Sisters Of Mercy	S L Wellings	16
My Black Void	Vicki Watson	17
Dog Food Is Awful	Joyce Walker	18
Chambercombe Manor	Wendy Watkin	19
Nightmares	Fran Vincent	20
Forever Tied Souls	Emma Jane Tomlinson	21
I'll Miss You So Much	April Twidale	22
Destitution	C Thornton	23
The Saviour In An Apron	Lachlan Taylor	24
Playground Tantrums	R N Taber	25
A Good Samaritan	Ellen Thompson	26
Robin Hood	Tony MacMillan	27
Statemented	Francis Mcdermott	28
On A Bright Sunny Day	Jean P McGovern	30
You Win Again	Steffen Ap Lloyd	31
A Wonderful Machine Is A Human Being's Hand	Erica Menzies	32
The Happy Room	P J Littlefield	34
Gamble	J Linehan	35
Wealth	Cecil J Lewis	36

Beautiful Stranger	Joe Loxton	37
Green, Green Grass Of Home	Ivy Lott	38
Trials	Marjorie Leyshon	39
Cherril's Resolve	Keith Leese	40
My Miracle	Daphne Young	41
Lymm May Queen	Daniel C Wright	42
Goodbye	Eric E Webb	43
If I Should Die	Edward Wall	44
E-Pals	Lisa Cresswell Wilkinson	45
The Lady Who Painted Her Dreams	Lindsey Withey	46
Death	Wendy Walker	48
Electric	Margaret Nixon	49
Lost Youth	Hilary Moore	50
Music	Vik	51
The Artist In The Sky	Joan McQuoid	52
Famine	Kim Montia	53
Sleeping Beauty	Gillian Mullett	54
National Symbols	Joy Morton	55
If Only	Hazel Mills	56
The Long Mourning	John Marshall	57
A City Proud	Malcolm Peter Mansfield	58
Feeling Good	Alma Montgomery Frank	60
Lines On Elliot	R H Rodger	61
For Someone Special	Rachel Rising	62
My Friends And Me	Sarah Robinson	64
The Inventor	Michael J Pritchard	65
Survival Of 1914-1918 War	Dorothy Rowe	66
Underpayments!	Daf Richards	68
A (Very Short) Evening With Oliver Reed	Brian L Porter	70
For Chris II	Angela G Pearson	72
New Year Honours - 2003	John Paulley	73
Angel	Gayna Florence Perry	74
Roche Abbey	Mary Parker	75
In Mine Eye	Tony Pitt	76
These Fragile And Flimsy Gifts	Jonathan Pegg	77
A Little Humour	Keith L Powell	78

My Gentle Giant	Margaret Pow	79
Royal Flush	Kathleen Potter	80
The Headmaster	Nicola Pitchers	81
My Stroke	Ivor Emlyn Percival	82
A Poem Dedicated To The West Pier	Yoshihiro Okumura	83
Painted Life	L O'Rourke	84
English Breakfast	Jon Oyster	85
Pride	Agnes Neeson	86
The Blacksmith	K S Nunn	87
A Poem	Giovanni Nacci	88
Little Willies	A Norton	89
Only Fools And Pantoums	Mick Nash	90
Graveyard	M M Graham	92
An Ode To The Queen Of The Street	Eileen Glenn	93
Decay	Margaret Gurney	94
A River Through Time	Jeanette Gaffney	95
WWW.When Will We See, Set Everyone Free.UK	Carl S Fricker	96
Bewitching Woman	Gary J Finlay	97
The Voice	Kerry Feild	98
Children	Imelda Fitzsimons	99
Through The Window	Josephine Foreman	100
Eleventh	Hugh Campbell	101
Black Widow	S Farley	102
A Teddy Bear's Picnic?	E M Eagle	104
Seventy	Jane England	105
The Seed Of The Soul	Andrea Darling	106
Your Ocean Love	Carol Ann Darling	107
My Worst Nightmare	Rosemary Davies	108
Nothing Learned	Paul David Dawson	109
The Magic Of Badbury Rings	Sammy Michael Davis	110
Dear Mum	Stephen Denning	111
Still	W A Ronayne	112
Inspiration	Frank Keetley	113
Tongue-Tied	Ailsa Keen	114
I Know You Know	Karla Kerr	115

Labyrinth Of Life	Sandra Kinnear	116
Tidy	C King	117
Without You	Donna Kane	118
Sticky Bun (Brimham Rocks, Near Ripley, Yorks)	Paddy Jupp	119
Insomnia	George S Johnstone	120
As I Look	Carol John	122
Mousey Thanks	E B Holcombe	123
What Makes Me Smile	Jane Margaret Issac	124
Memories	Maria Jenkinson	125
Punished With Pride	Graham Hare	126
Alter The Clocks	Kathleen M Hatton	127
Sympathy	Austin Healey	128
Friends	Elizabeth Hiddleston	129
Daylight	Kimberly Harries	130
Empty	Karl A Hunter	131
What Do You See?	Jo Hodson	132
Attitude Changes	R D Hiscoke	133
On The Theft Of A Friend	Susan Harwood	134
The Gainsborough Line	Steve Glason	135
Early, Early Musicals	Brian Benjamin	136
Is This The Answer To A Prayer?	Marie Barker	138
Bunny Rabbit's Seeds Of Life	Linda M Breeze-Gray	139
Changes	Gina Bowman	140
The Distance	J A Brown	142
Pickle	Eileen Burgess	143
The Castle	Lydia Barnett	144
The First Blink	John Andrews	145
Old Age	Thomas Ainsworth	146
For Amy	Andrew V Ascoli	147
Longing	Sarah Allison	148
Untitled	Philip Allen	149
No Oil Painting	Colin Allsop	150
Winner Takes All	Maureen Arnold	151
Swing Low	Arthur	152
It Takes Two	Pamela Carder	153
The Sailor	Mary Carroll	154
The Coal Place	Janet Cavill	155

You And Me	Walter John Coleman	156
Till Death Do Us Part	N Barry-Mills	157
My Mum	Jill Corkish	158
Encore	E Balmain	160
Abuser	Diane Blount	161
A Week Of Men	Sarah Blackmore	162
Lark Ascending	G Buckland-Evers	163
Just A Dream	Alan Brunwin	164
How We Love To Queue	A A Brown	165
Thank You For My Grandsons	Margaret M Donnelly	166
Holiday Tan Blues	J Alan Crook	167
Elsewhere	Lucy Crispin	168
Rising Up	Wendy Chaffer	169
We Play Out Part	C S Cyster	170
Another Year Gone	C J Walls	172
The Best Christmas Present Ever	Zoë Thompson	173
Not Gentle, Just Screaming	Helen R Eccles	174
Grandad, My Best Friend	Bee Wickens	175
Wise Parenting	Emmanuel Petrakis	176
Our Lodger	Cynthia Pitch	177
Company	Doreen Petherick Cox	178
I Wonder Why	Bethan Gifford	179
What's The Word I'm Looking For?	J L Copestake	180
Save Me (Cos I Love You)	Simon Cardy	182
Humility	Dennis Lye	183
A New Kind Of Warfare	Peter Asher	184
Eastertide	V J Askew	185
Captive	Maggy Copeland	186
A Simple Life . . .	Di Castle	187
When God Made Time . . .	Hilary J Cairns	188
Drop Of Pleasure	Harold Cotterill	189
Think Of Him	Kevin P S Collins	190
Hospital	Kinsman Clive	191

I Married A Comedian's Nightmare

My wife's a comic's nightmare,
Knows the end to every joke.
She loves to work out punchlines,
Then quote them while they talk.

No matter the occasion,
She doesn't seem to care.
Her quest to blurt out endings,
Drives me to despair.

Drastic means are needed,
If I'm ever to escape.
So I plan to tie her to the chair,
Then seal her mouth with tape.

If she proves too cunning
And thwarts me with a mime,
I'll simply turn her chair around,
To get some peace next time.

There she'll sit every night,
No chance of a remission.
Little scope for getting free,
Unless I choose to charge admission.

Paul Kelly

LAUGH OUT LOUD

If you think it's funny,
Laugh out loud.
Release your chuckle,
Stand up proud.
Don't hide your giggle,
Let it be.
Shed tears of happiness,
For the world to see.
If you grunt like a pig,
Then don't be shy.
Just keep laughing,
Until you cry.
Drop to your knees,
When your sides are split.
Roll over the floor,
With a laughing fit.

Laura Squibb

I'D RATHER NOT . . .

I'd rather not be a thinker
Than be a thinker who thinks
Sterile thoughts that wilt and die
In the womb of the invisible.

I'd rather not be a dreamer
Than be a dreamer who dreams
Castrated dreams that spoil
In the birth canal of yearning.

I'd rather not be a visionary
Than be a visionary who envisions
Miragic visions that disappear
The nearer to realising them I come.

I'd rather not be a speaker
Than be a speaker who speaks
Hollow sounding words that do not
Reflect the life I daily live.

For what is life if we do not
Live others to serve
And what is hope that does not
In Christ find its true fulfilment?

George Saurombe

ANGEL WALKING

I saw an angel walking upon a silicate sea
And she wore a flame-red halo in her walk of fantasy
Shimmering and gilded, she walked upon the glass,
And diamonds and carbons lay, where for aeons grew grass.

Ions and neutrons sparkle in the dark night
Occasionally refracting the slither of a chink of light.
Glittering and glistening in the dust that hides the day,
A light pulse from a diamond as on the ground it lay.

I saw angels walking dark mountains in the sky,
Ghosting in and out them, never to question why,
Steel and concrete mountains, the builders long since gone
Angels in their wandering the way they've always done.

Among the crags and rocks, and shapes of every kind
Unsymetrical, irregular, no need to be aligned
Spewed out from the earth bowels upon a world lay bare
And no inquisitive or clever mind will regulate them there.

I saw an angel walking down by a crater wide,
And the angel turned it to a lake with the tears she cried,
And the waters of the lake, began to ebb and flow,
So maybe in a million years, on these banks a flower will grow

Maybe in a thousand years the sky will once again be blue
The sun will shine on a cold, old world and form a drop of dew.
Then an angel will sit and sit with great aplomb,
Close to the very spot, where one man dropped a bomb.

George Speechley

IMAGINE

Imagine the very first snowdrop
Standing proud, in a carpet of snow
Imagine a field, full of buttercups
Like the brightest sunshine, they glow.

Imagine the laughter, of children
Their sweetness, their gentle touch
Imagine the love in someone's eyes
As they whisper, 'Thank you so much.'

Imagine my friend, with hair, like snow
Her smile, filled the room, with sunshine
Imagine her tiny, frail body
A little age'd hand, clasped in mine.

Imagine how I felt today
As I whispered, 'Goodbye' at the end.
Imagine the peace in Heaven
Sleep tight Enid, my wonderful friend
                            1909-2003.

Margaret Suffolk

WORKING MAN'S HAND/FEET

Working man's hand

Hardened calluses
  From work and toil
    Flattened fingerprints
     Ingrained with oil
      Fingers so strong
       Blue veins along
        Gentle but tough as sand
         Nothing so beautiful
          As a working man's hand

Working man's feet

Hardened yellow skin
From the strain and the pace
Bunions and corns
From the walk and the race
Nails hard and tough
Soles and heals rough
Untidy un-neat
Nothing so ugly
As working man's feet.

Gail Sturgess

WEARING OUT

My bones are weary
My eyes are dim
My hair is even going thin

My ankles swell
My knees both creek
And sometimes I can get no sleep

Cholesterol going up and down
My doctor shakes his head and frowns

My piles keep coming back as well
I wish that they would go to Hell

I'm always at the chemist door
To get prescriptions by the score

My back is knackered
And so are my teeth
I've even blisters on my feet

I thought that this would raise a smile
And keep you happy for a while.

Kathleen South

I HAVE LOVED THEE

I have loved thee since the world began,
Before night and day were separate,
Before God created man,
As the first cell divided into two
Thus commenced our destiny, was born my love for you.

I have loved thee since the world began,
No other woman loved like this
Within the earthly span.
No passion quite so deep as mine;
No face so fair, nor body sweet as thine.

I have loved thee since the world began.
Thou leaving me I bear as best I can;
And as my lonely way I wend
My heart repeats with every step,
I will love thee until the world doth end.

Thomas R Slater

UNIQUE

Shall I compare thee to a summer's day
Or a wet weekend?
Should I say you're like a rainbow
And follow you to the end?
Are you like an autumn leaf
Blowing free in the wind?
Are you like a scrap of rubbish
That I should have binned?
You remind me of a winter's morning
When you're frosty and cold
I don't even know your age
Are you young or old?
You are so changeable it seems
That you're a mystery.
You are my conscience, you know,
And you belong only to me.

Mary Anne Scott

UNTITLED

Would that I knew
My trust in thee
To be deserved?
Then great would be
The trust and love
I feel for thee
But doubts admittedly
Do prevail me
Torturous thoughts
Do still avail me
For trust is not born
Of empty shell
But must be learned
And nurtured well
So deeply I do pray
You show me well
Teach me the way
That I couldst dwell
And never stray
But love thee more
Each coming day.

N A Smith

ONLY YOU

May God! Grant us, a truly beautiful day,
With the heavenly sun, and moon, are in their play.
May the stars dance away above, your golden head,
As in all things, our strong love, is read.
I picture it among the great seas of the Earth,
As they murmur their satisfaction, for they know your worth.
I hope, your sensitive touch, blesses many a sandy shore,
For I wish to be with you, forever more!
All until, time itself, starts ticking backwards,
Or until, I'll be finally lost for mere words,
As you bring charm and grace, to the smallest birds.
While your light touch, opens the heads of beautiful flowers,
Yes! I could just sit and listen to you, all them lonesome hours.
What am I to do? For I am totally captivated,
Liken to a great cat, I am mindful, and fascinated.
Such wit, as there is delicate grace,
As I watch time spent, through the shining of your face.
You are as warm, like radiant sunshine,
And I am so glad, that you are truly mine!
For I don't know what I would do
If, I wasn't loving, only you!

Victor Shaw

DROWNING

If you have lifeboats prepare to launch them now,
I come to drown myself not to praise me.
For 40 years I have lived somehow
But never living up to what I could be.

The walking wounded and the waking dead
Deceived by an arrogant imagination
Thinking like Narcissus in my head
Putting the contempt in contemplation.

Hail Caesar, those about to die salute you
And those who've never lived sit idly by
Without ever the guts it took to shoot you
But drowning as the ides of March, march by.

Nic Scanlan

EINE KLEIN NACHT MUSIK
(Apologies to Mozart)

Cough, splutter, wheeze and fart
burp, moan and then
mutter, snore, gasp and choke
heck up a goodly load of phlegm.

Winkles tinkle on the floor
enough to float a boat
someone sitting fully dressed
in trousers, shirt and coat.

Moan, groan, swear and cuss
apologies to nurse
don't pick at that and put that down
you'll only make it worse.

Back to bed you naughty men
it's time for a cup of tea
please try not to ring that bell
what's that? You want a wee?

Cough, splutter, wheeze and fart
burp, moan and then
beep, beep, I want the bog
blimey, here we go again!

Roger Stevens

RAVELLO'S TRACK RECORD

On the mule track to Amalfi
drink iced lemon in Pontony
cools the ardour, so hot for love
best approach to town, from above.

Mule track to catch a boat, time flew
Minori to Amalfi, knew
must get bus to Ravello Square,
peace, with kids playing, life all fair.

Passing mule-train so made our day
as we walked to Minori Bay
the beasts return home their job done
up hill in this heat they could run.

Mule track which led us all the way
to Minori; what made us stay
was the Roman villa and bath
multi-time making this the path

Given fresh apricots, we were
by friendly peasants, had to stir;
draws us back to the mule track, sea
calling from Castiglione.

Robert D Shooter

LONELINESS

One or two about the place
There to fill the hours to face
To ease the strain, the loneliness
That would be great you would confess
A word or two about your day
To drive those thoughts that are glum away
A chair drawn up and put in place
A form to fill that empty space
A smile, a tear - whatever comes
To halt the constant twiddling of thumbs
On hands that sag without their need
With nowt to do to stop heart bleed
A voice to hear - to listen to
Company there to cheer up you
What could be a better thing
That could come to happiness bring
To those both old and on their own
Who understand that being alone
Destroys the heart, the will to live
The chance for once in faith to believe
One or two - about the place
Is to need such a big disgrace
Just the one would do and nothing less
To instil the hope - of happiness
How much more contented then one might be
If a friend could come - for company!

John L Wright

SISTERS OF MERCY

They locked me up at the age of twelve
Because of that man my belly swelled
Now they tell me it wasn't my fault
So why do I rot here while he grows old.

My education wasn't what it should have been
I didn't know what his attentions would bring
The church screamed out that it was a sin
But I didn't do anything.

Thirty years later I just stare at the walls
No spark of interest in life at all
Now the sister tells me I can leave
I can't imagine what she means.

They've let me out, I'm even more alone
Gave me money, gave me a home
They must think my heart's made of stone
But I just can't let go.

I'm older now but I still can't see
How being robbed of my innocence convicted me.
I lost my youth, it was torn away
Can't cope with life day to day.

I can't go back and trace my child
No records were kept, they've burnt all the files
There's nothing left out here for me,
It's either back to my priest or blessed release.

S L Wellings

MY BLACK VOID

I was lost in the darkness,
So alone, so afraid,
I failed to see the beauty before me,
I really had my life made.

Two beautiful children,
A partner who never ceased to care,
But I was too deep in the black void
To even realise they were there.

I found it a struggle to sleep,
I found it even harder to awake,
I couldn't face the day ahead,
I was putting everything at stake.

I had so much anger within,
I hated myself so bad,
I hurt the ones I loved so much,
Regretfully I was glad.

The pills they began to help me,
Suddenly the sun shone in again,
I began to smile genuinely once more,
I was finally getting rid of the pain.

Vicki Watson

DOG FOOD IS AWFUL

Dog food is awful
And I'll tell you why,
The missus once fed it
To me in a pie.

Dog food is awful
It doesn't taste sweet,
It's got animal bits
We humans don't eat.

Dog food is awful,
Or is it just offal?

Joyce Walker

CHAMBERCOMBE MANOR

Chambercombe Manor is spooky they say,
a ghost treads the boards in the night.
Is it a rumour? Or maybe a lie,
if you visit you're bound to find out.

Certain things happened in days long ago
things that I'm not sure are true,
someone was murdered, of that I do know,
but many will come here to view.

It's set in a picturesque meadow of green,
but the flowers do not always grow.
They say a young woman can often be seen,
wandering about to and fro.

The rooms are quite small, Tudor I believe,
one certain room holds a clue -
if someone's nervous they'll just have to leave,
I expect that's a thing some will do.

I hear there's a tunnel that leads to the sea,
where smuggling and such things occurred.
Ships did set sail to the beach - Rapparree -
where pirates held hostages on board.

Much comes to light of dark, daring deeds -
inside those dark, craggy caves.
As time goes by memories fade -
but what of those innocent slaves?

Reports have been made of wreckages found,
under those grey, murky waves,
valuable treasures - befitting a crown,
but many a soul lost their lives.

Wendy Watkin

NIGHTMARES

I closed my eyes yesterday, or was it last week?
I saw a long green beetle, it must have been three feet
And it jumped upon my stomach,
It started to eat
So I screamed.

I saw the door open wide so I tried to stand
But my legs were like jelly beans and I trod on my hand
And the beetle hung about my neck
So I screamed.

I heard my wife calling and she came through the door
Only she was not alone - she had multiplied to four.
I threw the green thing in the air
And it scuttled 'cross the floor
So I screamed.

I must have had too much to drink - was it yesterday?
I wish that horrid thing would go away
It sat upon my right big toe
And my foot went grey
So I screamed.

Fran Vincent

FOREVER TIED SOULS

When you told me you loved me,
It ran through my soul.
When your blue eyes longed for me,
They embedded a hold.

When you first called me Ems,
I was yours alone.
When you first caressed my body
I knew I'd found home.

My longing to be with you
Is always my pain.
My being without you,
Is a cloud without rain.

I feel your thoughts,
Though miles away.
You feel mine too,
No words have to say.

We are linked forever.
We can't say goodbye,
To the halves of each other,
We hold, still tied.

Nothing has untangled,
The knot we hold,
That binds us together,
Forever tied souls.

Emma Jane Tomlinson

I'll Miss You So Much

I did like you being there
But how can this be it?
It's the end of an era
I don't know what I'll do
Cos I'll miss you so much.

How will I ever cope
I don't know, but I'll try
I will try and find a way without you
I will never see your face
You were happy which kept me happy
And I'll miss you so much.

I will never ever hear you
Giving me good advice
You were always there
No matter what did happen
I'll miss you so much.

But now I'll have to try
Cos I'll never cope
So I might as well forget
And try and move on
I'll never forget you
Cos I'll miss you so much.

I will try and fight
The pain that's holding me back
Cos I will never see
Or know you anymore
I will try really hard to cope
But just remember this
Cos I'll miss you so much.

April Twidale (15)

DESTITUTION

Four million homeless, a tortured cry,
capitalist gift to profitless lie,
cheating, stealing, despised beast,
to curry fortune, demean the least,
a world of envy, favours few,
the masses expense, bewailing hue,
builders search for tolls to build,
gone to pay for councillors' guild,
legalised theft, the law it deemed,
to pass out sentence, innocent seemed,
lost and frightened, imposing court,
intimidate many, the fevered thought,
guilt inducement, falsely claim,
you are wrong! So take the blame,
the crime of poorness, chain our heart,
to walls of prisons, the pain to start,
at missing children, suffer the tears,
at wanton horror, coldeyed hears,
nothing but praises, laudable views.
A monster's seen, the Devil takes stock,
sharpens axe and readies the block.

C Thornton

THE SAVIOUR IN AN APRON

Our family know the debt we owe
and which we can never pay
for a mother who in nurturing us
worked doubly hard each day.

Father's health was never good
so it was on Mother we relied
and being determined in her ways
she struggled, toiled and strived.

We never had material things
as our budget did not cover
but we never went without our food
produced by our dear mother.

She always saw to her family's needs
just like a broody hen
and often missed out on herself
without a thought of where and when.

I would say that Mother was a saint
as she was the family's saviour
she kept our heads above the waves
with her indomitable behaviour.

Lachlan Taylor

PLAYGROUND TANTRUMS

Swing high, swing low,
kicking at the sky,
jerking to and fro
like a compass eye

Come to rest, time to leave,
dragging on a finger
signing from its sleeve,
we dare not linger

Things to do, places to see
between earth and sky,
besides gesturing rudely
at faces passing us by

Grown-ups pausing to play,
wishing the years away.

R N Taber

A GOOD SAMARITAN

A good Samaritan, as such, seldom craves a name
They seek no acclamation, nor do they ever claim
Attention from the media, just there to lend a hand
Whenever it is needed and seem to understand
The many ways of helping, a word, a smile, a touch,
A host of all those simple things which always mean so much.
It is an inborn instinct, this talent they possess,
Their greatest aim in life to give a taste of happiness
To those who seem to have none, weighed down by grief and woe,
Coping quite beyond them, with no get up and go,
Then someone kind, out of the blue, somehow just appears
Brings order out of chaos and wipes away the tears.
Should more than this be on the cards, they try to give advice
The current problems of our age not settled in a trice.
When those 'bigger guns' come in, the system put in place,
Our good Samaritan moves on to yet another place,
Just one of many nameless ones, I know of some don't you?
Here and now I sing their praise, acknowledgement is due.

Ellen Thompson

ROBIN HOOD

Robin Hood was a famous outlaw
Who robbed the rich to feed the poor
Not quite like Gordon Brown today
Who robs us all with a 'hoots wha hae'.

He went to live in a great big wood
No woman would join him, neither bad nor good;
But he needed a wife to do the carryin'
He got so cross - until he made Marian.

He lived for years then was ill in an abbey
And asked for his bow as he lay like a babby
He fired his last arrow and said to his men
'Bury me where it falls on hilltop or glen.'

So they buried him on top of the wardrobe.

Tony MacMillan

STATEMENTED

I cannot walk as fast as you or follow Miss in all she does
I cannot even tie my shoes or hear so well above the buzz
I cannot walk without a stick or play the climbing game
I cannot join the teams you choose or ever be quite the same
I cannot cry as you run away and laugh to meet your mother
I cannot go for I must stay to wait for someone or another.

Key stage two I grow too quick though I've little clue as I'm often sick

My teacher thinks that I don't know the clever words she read
My teacher sees no hurt I show when I cry inside my head
My teacher reads my statement plan seeing I'm not up to speed
My teacher feels beyond my span are words like education need
My teacher tries to understand what goes on inside my dignity
My teacher please just hold my hand, it helps to ease the agony.

Key stage three at last I learn my own identity I have to earn

I am the same as anyone and I can do the classroom task
I could share some silly fun you only have to ask
I could join your secret play and be your super friend
I could stand up (in a way) and my shoulder I would lend
I could always speak for you as others called you names
I remember how the jeering grew as I tried to play your games

Key stage four still feeling pain as a marginal equal I remain

Social worker I'm not a case try your best please don't evade
SENCO please look at my face I really need some learning aid
Special assistant look at me and talk to me please not at the ceiling
Head of Year I have got reason how do you know what I am feeling?
Psychologist it isn't contagious behaving like your words defined
Advocate eases my rages I cannot say what's on my mind

Older still FE remains indifferent to adolescent pains

Careers Advisor try to listen I am only human and get upset
My course tutor you are missing what I can offer (to my regret)
Senior lecturer give me some hope that I can learn with due respect
Head of School I'm trying to grasp a kind of life
                                                you cannot wreck
Divisional manager please accept that I am part of student life
College counsellor don't look bored I want to be somebody's wife

Doctor don't try to listen
I'm just too weak
Nobody heard
When I tried to speak
Look I hurt no more
And I have no sorrow
God knows where
I'll be tomorrow.

Francis Mcdermott

ON A BRIGHT SUNNY DAY

Here in Carshalton, when the days are bright
Two swallows are seen, as they take flight
Their twittering warble tones and varying voice
Produced on the wing, are their songs of rejoice

A mile away stands a beautiful park
Where melodic liquid phases, sounds from a lark
Building a neat cup nest, upon the ground
Built by both members, hardly making a sound

In the park two graceful swans, glide to and fro
Where the peace and hope, of the rivers gently flow
Such a pictures when the sun comes smiling through
When clouds unfold, and the skies turn blue

Further on, ducks and geese are seen
While the grebe sings, his wailing song, upon the green
Laying her seven eggs, in the early month of May
Protected by both parents, are the chicks across the way

Further on church bells ring out merrily
Bringing a contrast through the ecstasy
Just imagine the peace, with its surroundings
Making the days bright, as each bird sings

Especially the quiet sounds, of the willow warbler
A pleasant whistle sounds, with the song of the swallow
Flapping their wings, as they glide up to the sky
Their voices are distinctive, a pitch voice so high

If visiting Carshalton, where the best things are free
Especially on a bright day, where it holds such beauty
Until the day turns to the shadows of the night
When the white, beautiful swans shine, under the moonlight.

Jean P McGovern

YOU WIN AGAIN

I waited for your answers
I waited all in vein,
you left me there to suffer
and to carry all this pain.
Your love for me was absolute
there was never no redress,
then you took your love away from me
and left me in this mess.
You left me with this heartache
you left me with the pain,
you had me back then left me
and you did it all again.
They say only fools go back for more
for me I know it's true,
what hurts me most deep down inside
is that I was fooled by you.
Now I'll never get my answers
and I think you've made it plain,
that smile of yours it says it all . . .
you win again.

Steffen Ap Lloyd

A Wonderful Machine Is A Human Being's Hand

Four fingers and a thumb
Can lift a fallen chum
Or hold neat rum
A Jew's harp strum
A human being's hand

Four fingers and a thumb
Can drive a nail in straight
Put coals upon the grate
Bring account books up to date
Drive a car at quite a rate
A human being's hand

Four fingers and a thumb
They can build a house of stone
Also fetch the dog a bone
Help to lick an ice cream cone
Comfort a widow when she's alone
A human being's hand

Four fingers and a thumb
Can plant seed in the ground
Hold back a lively hound
From a piano flows a pleasant sound
Or bind up a bleeding wound
A human being's hand

Four fingers and a thumb
With them fly an aeroplane
Maybe gather much dishonest gain
Hold a brolly in the rain
Make a box, bits and pieces to contain
A human being's hand

Four fingers and a thumb
Jesus' hands were of the best
His - brought a stormy sea to rest
With His hand in ours we're blest
Warms our heart - deep in our chest
A Saviour's nail pierced hand

Four fingers and a thumb
When our Lord's hand opens Heaven's gate
May none of us be late
He will not forever wait
Come now whate'er your state
Feel that grip so intimate
A Saviour's nail pierced hand

A little, final thought

Four fingers and a thumb
This poem of sorts has grown
A few lines, just some
From the author's dad did come
Others really an added crumb
It does prove, don't be dumb

A wonderful machine
Is a human being's hand.

Erica Menzies

THE HAPPY ROOM

To lift my load,
In these days of gloom,
Often I let myself in,
To that special room,
You know the place,
Deep in a hidden corner of your mind,
It's passed tragedy and turmoil,
It's where peace and beauty I can find,
Immediately I am met,
By happy moments and laughter's glow,
Of sunny days in flaming June,
Many, many years ago,
That was when we met,
And you stole my heart,
And from that day to this,
We've never been apart,
Your elegance and beauty,
Your pose and grace,
Engulfed me totally,
Filling my empty space,
That's how it's been,
Contentment has been our key,
Taking each day as it comes,
With grandchildren on your knee,
But tomorrow things will change,
Because I will slip away from you,
To the next life I am bound,
I'll go in peace, to meet my end,
But I will stay close by, not far away,
Not far from your spectrum will I stray.

P J Littlefield

GAMBLE

I've let you into my life
And put my feelings on the line
Will we turn out all right?
Have I took a wrong gamble this time

The odds are 50/50
No favourites or 100-1
I didn't want us to get serious
It started just as fun

Is my horse a winner?
Will we make the last felon?
Will we jump all the hurdles?
Will we hit the line head on?

The finish line is so far away
But in the horizon I can see
You and me getting on so fine
Winners will both be

So it's 50 to you and 50 to me
Champions we both are
Because we made it to the end
Even though the race was far!

J Linehan

WEALTH

For fame and fortune people sigh
And dream of worldly wealth
But all the money cannot buy
The blessing of good health.

The legs and feet with which we walk
Bright eyes to see so clear
The voice and tongue with which to talk
And ears with which to hear.

It cannot buy a simple smile
Or a cheery word for you
And all the wealth man can compile
Can't buy a heart that's true.

Love is not bought, it has no price
Yet neither is it free
A gladly given sacrifice
That's wealth enough for me.

Cecil J Lewis

BEAUTIFUL STRANGER

Beautiful stranger, in your prime
Your face is lost in the mists of time
I used to see you every day
And thought your image was here to stay
But all of that is in the past
Somehow I knew it wouldn't last
Perhaps one day I will recall
That beautiful stranger who did enthral.

Joe Loxton

GREEN, GREEN GRASS OF HOME

I lean on farmyard gate
Gaze at panoramic view
Coppice green, lush glade
Beauty of early morn dew
My homecoming a 'welcoming'
Rural charm all around, still fascinating.

I tread early morn dew
Green, green grass of home
Only images in mind, no view
Whilst globetrotting to a'roam
Hopeful of love, more money, success
In this fleeting time of ours, to impress.

I left my beloved countryside to yearn
Key in lock now, I'm aware of homefire burning
Relaxed, warm, soul's ease to know
Memories sweet all returning
Peace, happiness, mine overflows
Ne'er again a'roaming I will go.

Ivy Lott

TRIALS

Some mornings you awaken feeling low and oh so blue
You wonder why it's happening and is it only just to you
And also hope the hours will brighten as your chores get underway
Then wish a pleasant issue will come along this day
You knock upset and drop things, everything falls to the floor
The frustrations seem so endless you agree with Murphy's Law.

Your morning toast goes sailing off course, it's butter side down
And then you spill some coffee down your brand new dressing gown
You wash the breakfast dishes, wouldn't you know you chip a cup
The lather of the soap suds have already wet your cuff
The cleaner hose keeps knocking you as you move across the floor
It is ever so annoying, turn, and bang into a door.

The polish and the duster just slips behind a chair
You puzzle how that happened also how it got just there
You bend down to retrieve them, you cannot believe your luck
And now it seems you cannot get up, your arm is really stuck
Then think, that's it, I'm frazzled, my nerves are really shred
The best thing I can think of, take a book and retire to bed.

Marjorie Leyshon

CHERRIL'S RESOLVE

She's a resolute lady, she certainly knows her own mind,
that's not to say she's hard-hearted, not to say she's unkind.
A self-reliant woman, just another victim of man's deceit,
hardened and resourceful, now standing on her own two feet.

A determined lady, bringing powerful views to life's debate,
saddling God with life's misfortunes, those little twists of fate.
A passionate woman, self cocooned from any further pain,
not to be tempered, not until she stops giving God the blame.

A spirited lady, her battle with God has reached the final show,
God's love is not for losing, compassion strikes the fatal blow.
Broken but made whole, those chains loose, her heart set free,
still a spirited lady, but walking now with the Lord of eternity.

Keith Leese

MY MIRACLE

From high on the cliff I gazed at that seat -
You were gone from me, we'd never meet.
Then with flash of gold that lit up the sky -
Out came the sun and hovered on high.

Right above that seat where you loved to be,
Sheltered by cliffs and close to the sea.
I felt you knew I would walk that way
Happiness is mine and it's here to stay.

The tears I shed will be of gladness,
Even though they be tinged with sadness -
Somewhere darling, you are there,
Somewhere and I know you care.

My second miracle (9 months later)

I felt I must walk to that dear old place -
Have courage to look at that empty space
Hadn't my friend suggested I go?
Why, she'd said that - I wanted to know!

Nothing prepared me for what I saw!
Bright yellow daffodils - more, more and more!
All round the cliff where I'd stood months ago -
The daffodils of our love's early glow.

I stood there and cried like a child today -
My flowers, your love
    Are with me, always.

Daphne Young

LYMM MAY QUEEN

These are the people and these are the places,
These are the names and these are the faces.

This is the crowd and this is us,
Feel the noise and feel the buzz.

Stand on the cross or stand at the front,
Be a witness and bear the brunt.

The parade goes on through the streets,
There's friends to see and people to greet.

Then she arrives, Queen for this year,
What a nice girl and oh what a dear.

Her beauty is spread throughout the crowd,
The people are pleased and her family are proud.

These are the people and these are the places,
These are the names and these are the faces.

Daniel C Wright

GOODBYE

So quiet, so peaceful, there was hardly a sound
As he left in the morning for his daily round.
He knew they were tired and deep in their sleep
His lips brushed their cheeks as he made his last peep
At the family he treasured - for him still they yearn,
If only they had known he was not to return.
Gone is his smile - his gentle touch
His acts of kindness which meant so much
To all who came near - each loved one and friend
All bewildered and shocked by his untimely end.
The sickening sound of a motorway crash
A dear life extinguished - snuffed out in a flash.
Robbed of goodbyes to friends left behind
And the touch of his loved ones to know peace of mind.
But the sweetest of memories will ever remain
A mixture of gladness garnished with pain.
And now as he slumbers in God's given peace,
Granted frail bodies at the end of their lease;
Those who are left to continue their story
Believers in Christ - in God's power and His glory
In time they will share what has long been concealed
The mystery of life which in death is revealed.

Eric E Webb

IF I SHOULD DIE
(Thoughts by Gavrelle Blanche Wall 1917-2003)

I know that when I breathe my last
The future beckons, gone is the past.
I need no coffin, just a shroud.
No mourners, just a cheerful crowd
Of those who loved me in my life,
Those to whom I caused no strife.
No speeches, cards, exotic flowers
That last for just the fleeting hours.
I will have gone, and I will wait
For those I love at Heaven's Gate.

Edward Wall

E-PALS

Apart we are ten thousand miles
Together we share a thousand smiles
Each day I know you're there for me
And I am too as you can see
No flesh to see no face to stare
In spirit and presence I know that you care
When I'm alone or feeling blue
In this cosy attic I meet with you
Your picture propped here by my side
As I open up to you and confide
On you I know I can truly depend
When you contacted me
I found a true friend.

Lisa Cresswell Wilkinson

THE LADY WHO PAINTED HER DREAMS
(For Marian Lacy)

She reached deep down into her core,
Blurred out reality,
She painted it as something more,
In misty fantasy.

She walked within this fairytale,
Where love was free to grow,
Where clouds were lilac, soft and pale,
The sun was indigo.

White larks sang tunes so clear and fair,
From canopies of green,
She lay down, free, without a care,
And soaked up this dream scene.

A river flowed past, calm and cool,
Aqua fresh with gold swirls,
She plunged into this nature pool,
Her real life unfurls.

The air is heady with jasmine,
Intoxicating scent,
But this is far from any sin,
This is what heaven meant.

She feasted on sweet wild berries,
Juice staining her fingers,
And orchard fruits; apples, cherries,
Her mellow mood lingers.

She picked a bunch of wild flowers,
Red poppies, pink sweet peas,
She sat amongst them for hours,
Green grass stains on her knees.

Soon came her alarm, bleeping feint,
Bringing on a new day,
And she knew just what she would paint;
All she'd dreamt whilst she'd lay.

Lindsey Withey

DEATH

How would you know if you were dead,
Do things stop going through your head,
Do you vanish into the sky above,
Or do clouds engulf you with their love?

To be at peace within yourself,
Is worth far more than all the wealth,
When your soul rises up far above,
The angels will show to you their love.

A perfect harmony there will be,
On looking down on the things we'll see,
Friends and loved ones carry on,
But all so sad now that you have gone.

Wendy Walker

ELECTRIC

I'd like to be electric,
I'd find it fun you see
To switch my current on or off
To make a cup of tea.

I'd like to be electric
And switch myself to go,
Recharging all my batteries
To give myself a glow.

I'd like to be electric
With a megawattic smile,
Enchanting those around me
With my latest lively style.

Or I could be a live wire
And give you shocks at night.
I could be a glowing fire
Or a bright and dazzling light.

And when I'm very angry
I could simply blow a fuse,
And set the sparks a-flying
Just anywhere I choose.

I know I'd be eccentric
But wouldn't it be fun
Becoming all electric
And powerful like the sun.

Margaret Nixon

LOST YOUTH

The laughing child grows up
Leaves home and takes on an
Independence of
His own.

Where then did he find the
Need to inject substances into
His body? To
Cope with studies and
The stresses of his life.

Just a thin, frail, sad
Dead adult.
Life wasted by
Class A drugs
Sold by greedy, evil men.

Wilted flowers and
Grieving parents are
All that is left of the
Laughing child.

Hilary Moore

MUSIC

Feel the beat
The instruments meet
Body trapped in motion
What a potion

Delivering the supreme pleasure
I just can't measure
Every muscle enhanced with cadence
Untainted euphoria immense

Heart pounding
Joints never floundering
The mind descends
Into rapture, music amends

Brain tingling craving more
There is no flaw
Tunes forever drumming
I could not live without its strumming

The essence of my passion
Embraces the perception
Melody is sole therapy
To life, to love, sadness and imagery

A song for every thought
Eyes shut all instruments caught
Mind-blowing . . . lyrics combining
The sincerity to living

Mine to be shared
Nothing compared
To a life with song
Don't wait too long.

Vik

THE ARTIST IN THE SKY

Each day the sky seemed bleak and grey
Until one evening - I must say.
The sky, it was the palest blue
And many clouds were pink in hue.
I really think when artists die,
Each one takes turns to paint the sky.
Now if it is a wintry day
The colours they won't be so gay.
But if the sun is shining bright,
The artists know which colour's right.
And this gives all of us below
When looking up, an inward glow.

Joan McQuoid

FAMINE

I am the stench attracting every fly
Around me, crops for miles, all withered dry
I am the swollen bellies and the tears
A mother's nightmare; what each father fears
I am the empty grain store and the bread
That hungry children dream about in bed
Desperation, shallow graves and death
Weakness and a prayer on every breath
I am those cries for mercy in the dark
And nothing but the truth where devils hark
From this inhuman tragedy I feed
I'm famine and I answer no one's need.

Kim Montia

SLEEPING BEAUTY

To a good king and queen one morn, a lovely baby girl was born
At her christening fairies came, and their many gifts they gave
Peace and happiness they bestowed, as the many blessings flowed
Laughter, beauty and dancing feet and for her good a nature so sweet

Then suddenly came a mighty bang that terrified them as it rang
The wicked fairy Grunhilda there stood,
Looking so evil as only she could
Her invitation had not been sent this, oversight had not been meant
She gave a curse as punishment, that the baby's life was spent

She left them in a cloud of smoke her wicked spell could not be broke
But the fairies used their power, to turn death to long sleep in a tower
On her sixteenth birthday she went to explore,
The turrets locked behind tall doors
And there Grunhilda beckoned her near to spin the thread, without fear

Her finger pricked the princess slept for a hundred years her secret kept
Then a handsome prince came to find,
If a princess slept in the castle confined
To where she lay he did his duty then knelt beside his sleeping beauty
With one gentle kiss she opened her eyes,
Their love was born, the castle revived
Great bells peeled out on their wedding morn,
Their happiness sealed for one and all.

Gillian Mullett

NATIONAL SYMBOLS

Thistle - emblem of the northern Gaels;
Land of the drums and the bagpipe wails.
The call of the homeland never fails.

The wild Welsh chose the daffodil;
They with harpsong the valleys fill;
The comfort of rugged mountains still.

The shamrock belongs to the Emerald Isle,
The Irish bagpipes sigh for mile upon mile:
The sounds of lament remain all the while.

The English boast the humble dog-rose.
The fiddle uplifts from sorrows and woes.
The symbols of home as everyone knows.

Joy Morton

IF ONLY

Wonder if she's there again,
Through the old, cracked windowpane,
Peering at the murky night
From house, so dim, with little light.

I saw her on my way to work;
Behind lace curtains, oft' she'd lurk.
Wonder who she's looking for,
No footsteps ever reach her door.

How old she is, I cannot tell.
Pale face, so lined, and far from well.
Must look for her this dismal night;
Alas, she is nowhere in sight.

I really must knock on her door
Or will she think I'm just a bore.
What if I call and no one's there?
At least I've shown I really care.

Came home from work again last night;
Passed by her house, there was no light.
Her curtains now are tightly drawn.
The house looks empty and forlorn.

Today, at last, approached her door.
'She does not live there anymore.'
And as I sadly turned away,
I knew I'd failed to seize the day.

Hazel Mills

THE LONG MOURNING

For an infinite second
The high point sustained
Ere down the long mourning
Our journey arraigned.

To pass then reflect
Over fading blooms
So as blood spills
From countless empty rooms
Do we understand reasons
For the pain we cause
Fast approaching some zenith
Maybe if we pause
Steal a few glances
Overtime half spent
Regain lost moments
From the rest half lent
Till down the long mourning
Only evening can comprehend
We waste the brief day
Leaving just dreams to tend

For the short journey
Our high point arraigned
Ere time infinite
The long mourning sustained.

John Marshall

A CITY PROUD
(For all friendly-faced Merseysiders 'red or blue')

A city proud, are we
Our heritage, is there
For all the world to see.

On the waterfront, alone
We have the graces, one, two, three.

Separated on a street called Hope
A cathedral or two
Graced by the presence of Queen and Pope.

Flanking a park named Stanley
Football grounds that bring delight
To our humour and sporting family.

Theatres, museums, galleries . . .
For all their fame
So many to mention and to name.

Though viewed from the one radio tower
The building of buildings
Possessing real pulling power:
'St George's Hall'
A public venue for everyone to recall.
Magnificent in splendour . . .
Grand with true artistic design . . .
The focus of all that is 'us' and benign.
Now a constant film star
The main attraction
Courting the tourist's heart
Both near and far.

Though the best advertisement
For this special place . . .
Is the smile and warm welcome
Of a friendly face.

Malcolm Peter Mansfield

FEELING GOOD

Waking up every morning feeling full of high spirits
It's just wonderful to behold
Singing the latest love song in your bath
Is sunshine at its best
Clicking one's heels on the way to the car
Telephoning one's friend to let them know you'll be there
Keeping others happy telling jokes all day
Coming back home to the family
Still full of happy thoughts and deeds
Dinner cooked in the healthy grill
It is over before you know why
Feeling good shines upon your loving face
Eating well, exercising well, sleeping well, feels good
And you will always be feeling good.

Alma Montgomery Frank

LINES ON ELLIOT

Sleek he lies beneath the water,
his brown back supple and taut
as a watch spring.
Bruises and cuts camouflage his flanks,
this tiger who is my son.
Fearless, ready to try,
enviously free of anxiousness,
how sometimes I wish he knew
what it is like to feel scared,
to taste the dry mouth,
to feel the chill of sweat.
His smile is as broad
as his thoughtful, caring mind.
His hands caverns of generosity.
But it is his eyes,
those magic fires that burn orange green
and grow in his imagination,
that reveal the tiger
is my son.

R H Rodger

FOR SOMEONE SPECIAL

When I looked at him I felt I'd known him all my life;
He told me he felt the same way.
When we looked into each other's eyes,
We were in our own little world,
And no one could take us away.

One night he took me to a different place
A place I'd never been.
We flew past the moon,
Went soaring past the stars
I could barely believe what I'd seen.

We sat upon the moon rock
To savour the glittering view
When he reached out his hand,
And he gave me a star,
And he said, 'Because I love you.'

When I had said goodnight,
I put my star upon the table
I remembered the stars
I remembered his eyes
It was as if it had all been a fable.

But then as a storm brewed one evening
He arrived at my door
He was leaving tonight
To a distant land
He couldn't have told me before.

As we held each other for one last time,
I remembered the words he had said.
He cried, I cried,
He gave me one last kiss.
Then he was gone next morning,
Travelling afar.

But in my dreams I always see him
With me, soaring past the stars.
In my heart there's always a place
For him, forever and ever.
I'll keep this star he gave to me,
And everywhere, and anywhere,
There he'll be.

Rachel Rising

MY FRIENDS AND ME

Three years ago, apart from some months,
I was alone in the raging sea.
A very small fish, enveloped and lost,
When a huge wave came to torment me.
This big white horse, it trampled and roared
And would not let me go free.

I screamed, I shouted and I pleaded,
'Won't somebody please, please rescue me?'
I could not escape, I floundered and wept,
I wanted to have fun and be free
From this terror, bewilderment, too.
I cried out, 'Just leave me be!'

Suddenly, from way over the cliff top,
Walking some of my friends, one, two and three.
Maybe more, I cannot say, I don't know.
Then they threw in a branch from a tree.
They pulled and they tugged, they did not stop.
I swam from the cruel sea.

They helped, cajoled, they made me see sense.
Their words were like honey from a bee.
They could have stopped, could have gone on their way.
But, no, they found the time and saved me.
I'd wanted to sink, accept my fate,
But my friends did not agree.

So if they read this, which I hope they will,
I'd like to say to all, honestly,
Thank you for caring, for showing me strength.
Thanks for giving me those cups of tea!
You helped me to survive through it all,
And to accept the true me!

Sarah Robinson

THE INVENTOR

Mr Franklin, Benjamin to his friends,
A statesman yes but an inventor sure.
A science genius I have no doubt,
Shown a problem he produced a cure.

Most daring had to be the lightning rod,
For in a thunderstorm he flew a kite
To show how lightning passed down a wire.
Already clever, this could have made him extra bright.

Michael J Pritchard

SURVIVAL OF 1914-1918 WAR

When Dundalk Road was a cinder path
And the kids used to run and play and laugh
There were railway sleepers built as a fence
To help World War One soldiers earn a few pence
Their families all gone, killed in the war
So allotments were given to grow their own food
Two legged stools were made with great care
Tables and chairs, so very rare,
Even their beds went into the walls
And houses they built without any halls
They built seventy more side by side
And they grew their own veg, and bought chickens.
They watched with pride, as the veg grew and the eggs were laid
When Katie and I visited,
Breakfast was made, with buttered toast
And two eggs apiece, we licked our lips,
'Oh what a feast!'
The eggs were sold or traded with friends
And of course wire meshing, to protect the hens
My friend's Uncle Tom was never mean
He was always clean shaven, and spotlessly clean,
Their washing would dry, dancing in the breeze
As some of the men planted, some digging
And some on their knees,
Because again the veg sold at the country fair
Helped them build better houses with great care
The timber yards were very good,
To build their houses they gave them some wood,
Visitors 'God love them' they had none
But when Katy and I called
We were always made welcome
But he was her uncle when all's said and done
All this started in 1919.

By 1933 we had reached our teens
My friend Katy died at the age of sixteen
Her tonsils gave way, and it's sad to say
They didn't know then what they know today.
Her friend was now gone
And she now felt she couldn't visit her friend's uncle Tom
Tis another part of history
That to many is a mystery
Mum died at 84, tis a shame I didn't find out much more.

Dorothy Rowe

UNDERPAYMENTS!

The equivalent of one penny,
that's what the third world gets
for growing our food, making our clothes,
they never get out of debt!

They wade in the paddy fields
from dawn until dusk,
get muddy and hot, slushy and wet,
then eat up the waste and the husk.

When growing our tea or our coffee
they fare even worse than that,
drink filthy water, diseases are rampant,
they're lucky to sleep on a mat.

Let's look at the clothes we wear.
Young girls work fingers to bone.
They never go out, don't have any fun
and their families leave them alone.

The young lads who weave our carpets
to help feed their families,
don't go to school, can't read or write,
and *never* earn any fat fees.

I've taken a few little items
to show how the *real* world lives.
No water on tap, no toilets indoors,
little cash for the time that they give.

In the west we take things for granted.
We don't worry about those in need.
We want this or that, two holidays a year,
don't think of the workers who bleed.

Try putting yourself in their place,
experience hardship, dust and flies,
then shop where you can get better-deal goods,
don't support those conglomerate lies.

Daf Richards

A (VERY SHORT) EVENING WITH OLIVER REED

Christmas at the Regent Hotel, the dinner had been a success,
The men resplendent in their finest suits, the ladies in seasonal dress.
Replete with fine food, and caressed by fine wines,
Palates sated, and with great bonhomie,
The party retired to the small intimate bar,
Where the talk and the drink flowed quite free.
As the evening wore on, so the revelry grew,
A fine time was being had by all.
And the goodwill of Christmas flowed ever more freely,
Everyone was having a ball.

And now, the time came, when once again,
Many glasses required refilling,
Four volunteers approached the bar, eager, ready and willing.
As the order they placed for drinks a'many,
The door to the bar opened wide,
And there, in person was Oliver Reed, who proceeded to stagger inside.
It seemed that Olly had perhaps imbibed,
A glass of Christmas spirit or two,
With his friend for support he approached the bar,
We wondered what he would do.

At the crucial moment, before reaching support,
He staggered, and before he could stop,
He clattered quite hard into poor Lorraine,
And her drink she promptly dropped.
And then, in a flash, there came a transition,
A wonderful change took place,
And Olly became the great Oliver Reed,
And he spoke, a serious look on his face.
'My lady,' said he, 'I am so very sorry,
Please forgive me, I implore you.'
Lorraine, taken aback could do naught but reply,
'I forgive you, of course I do.'

Once again he spoke in that distinctive voice,
'Allow me to replenish your drink,
For that one is empty, due to me, it's the least I can do I think.'
Lorraine accepted his offer with grace of course,
And before he took his leave,
He bowed like the great musketeer that he played in the movie,
And it was easy to believe,
That here was a man with more than one face,
But which was the real Oliver Reed?
Was it the man who first entered the bar,
Of he who performed the chivalrous deed?

As he left the door he'd so recently entered,
We sat huddled together at our table,
We spoke of the scene in which we'd all just played,
And, as best we were able,
We tried to separate the truth from the fiction,
To see beyond the obvious facts,
But could we ever have disseminated reality
About one who lived his life in acts?
We were of course fans of the actor, the man,
So the spirit of Christmas we did heed,
And to this very day, we all fondly recall,
Our short evening with Oliver Reed.

Brian L Porter

FOR CHRIS II

I feel a sense of loss, but it is not lost.
I cannot grieve for something that is still here.
Put away the pain,
else there is no gain
and friendship will pay the cost.

I reach out my hand, across the lands
and hope that you can still reach out to me.
In friendship true,
there's no need to feel blue,
because we will only do what we can!

Angela G Pearson

NEW YEAR HONOURS - 2003

November letter, facts so clear,
Treat in private, shield from Dear;
Think and dream of news so great,
Seven weeks, a frightening wait.

Final hours before news pact,
Call from press to check on facts;
Still no word to loving wife,
First great secret through our life.

Day arrived with no more waits,
Early call with lots of dates;
Joy and praise in cards and calls,
Was this the greatest day of all?

Throughout the day the phone just rang,
From near and far the praises sang;
The papers all contained some news,
With some there were some personal views.

One greater day we now await,
As car descends on Palace gates;
To meet our Queen in Palace hall,
'Twill be the greatest day of all.

To countless friends I owe so much,
Their words and work keep me in touch;
Without appeals and schools to aid,
Then life for me would quickly fade.

This honour from our glorious Queen,
Just does so much to keep one keen;
For loving wife, so loyal she's been,
A lifetime thrill, to meet our Queen.

John Paulley

ANGEL

I'd lie awake, making shapes from cracks in the ceiling;
I'd close my eyes, and recognise a beckoning feeling;
Take me back to that familiar place;
I'll go to inner space if I can see your face;
And when I get there, if I want to stay,
Will you be there next day, or will you go away?

My archangel's gone missing: oh, Michael, where are you?
It seems that something I should see is just beyond my view.
Gabriel or Raphael or Uriel would do;
I looked to find you in the sky, but you were missing too.
Oh, Angel, where are you? Where are you?

I know what you had told me; your warnings all came true;
I swear I'll listen this time; oh, Angel, where are you?
I fell in love with something that simply wasn't there
I kept on pushing open doors to find nothing but air;
Oh, Angel, where are you? Where are you?

I tell myself though I feel empty inside, I'm just fine;
But though I know that I can life and breathe, can I shine?

My archangel's gone missing: oh, Michael, where are you?
Are you right there for me to see yet just beyond my view?
And do you watch me looking, the thought of you in mind,
Not even knowing how to seek, not knowing what I'll find?
Oh, Angel, where are you? Where are you?

I know what you have told me; I know that it is true;
I only have to look with love to guide myself to you.
And if and when I find you, my doubts can disappear;
I can stop pushing open doors; my angel is right here;
Oh, Angel, where are you? Where are you?

Gayna Florence Perry

ROCHE ABBEY

Stark outline mutilated by age, weather and plunder,
Graceful arches of stone convey the mystery and wonder.
The history is there among the neatly trimmed lawns,
A complete Cistercian way of life by monks, mourned.

The quiet unnatural stillness is unique to this place,
Culture, serenity, calmness, obscured from the race.
Carpets of snowdrops planted by some bygone hand,
Wild daffodils, tossing their heads, claiming the land.

Among the ruins the water gurgles softly, whispering
Of a meditative life, long ago, beyond our imagining.
The swish of monks habits and the murmur of prayer
The gentle acknowledgement, they know we are there.

Mary Parker

IN MINE EYE

No rose has been created,
That with her beauty can compare,
Its scent pales in comparison
To the fragrance of her hair,

Her delicate skin, so petal soft,
As fine as smooth porcelain,
Never have I seen a beauty like her,
And, probably never will again,

With a finely structured body,
And shoulders a model's dream,
She walks with poise and dignity,
The epitome, of what is good and clean,

Her smile bathes all, in warmth and brightness,
She has humour unsurpassed,
Should you win the love that she can give,
Throughout your life, this love will last,

If foolish enough to offend her,
And be the object of her wrath,
You will not have her trust again,
For she never does things by half.

Tony Pitt

THESE FRAGILE AND FLIMSY GIFTS

He bestows upon me little gifts.
I ask him why do I warrant this?
He says I give him treasures unseen.
Their meaning he is to make clear.
This day he comes to me,
With little pots of newly sprouted ferns
Maiden hair, lady fern and hart's tongue,
Half a dozen species it appears.
What a strange token of friendship.
This gift he carries a precious cargo.
So filmy and fragile,
Seemingly not built for survival.
Not able to stand the sunlight glare.
Born in places of damp and shade.
Some fairy dell or woodland glade.
Amongst the stones of a ruined monastery,
Where they modestly make their home
Grow lacy canopies which bear no seeds.
So old, they breed from rusty spores,
Scatter on the forest's mould rich floor.
These plants, almost as old as time
First grew in the primordial forests,
Their fossil stems we now burn as coal.
He tells me he gives me these gifts.
These time-rich flimsy things.
To him they are a friendship ring.
For in truth he says, they're heaven-sent
As they are as old as our immortal souls.

Jonathan Pegg

A LITTLE HUMOUR

It was just a little humour
Just a little joke
But it got a little out of hand
And ended up in smoke.

It was just a little humour
To get us all to laugh
But it has really gone wrong
And here we are looking and feeling daft.

It was just a little humour
So we must take more care
And make sure in the future
Someone is always there.

Keith L Powell

MY GENTLE GIANT

He lies beside me
Closes his eyes
Drifts away
To fantasise

No more motion
He's at peace
Though his breathing
Does not cease

Oh so still
Oh so calm
This can only
Describe my man

Hand on heart
Hand on head
Oh so tired
Needs his bed

Very warm
To the touch
Snoring loudly
In fact too much.

Margaret Pow

ROYAL FLUSH

Purple I'll wear when I'm old
declaration that I've grown bold
like a plum, juicy, delicious
senior turned capricious
flaunting charms in gown of purple
smile demurely then turn turtle.
Play bingo, dance from dusk till dawn
paint the town red till early morn
creep to bed, sleep twenty-four hours.
Cleanse, make-up, go buy some flowers
an offering of benediction
penance for pain and frustration.
Peace restored, face wreathed in smiles
jump a train that eats up the miles
on vacation, find a patron
who'll wine and dine me on Stilton.
A different town in purple gown
I'll find a man who'll laugh and clown
we'll roar our way round the globe
return a confirmed Anglophobe.
Breakfast on whiskey, fish and chips
till breath fails to pass from my lips.
Coffined in my long purple robe
smile as bright as a laser strobe.

Kathleen Potter

THE HEADMASTER

Today was the first day of school, and I met my new headmaster,
I knew from the first few moments this day would be a disaster.
The headmaster introduced himself and asked us to do the same,
but I got really nervous and couldn't pronounce my name.
Everyone started laughing and made my face go red,
I got the strangest feeling I should have stayed in bed.
The headmaster started to talk, about how good this school could be,
as long as we knuckled down because discipline was the key.
He says he's the man he is today, because he did well at school,
he hung around the library instead of the playground trying to be cool.
Everything was going okay until someone kicked my chair,
I fell flat on my face right under the headmaster's glare.
I smiled my award winning smile, but it didn't do any good,
he dragged me to face the wall on the stage, and totally embarrassed,
                                          that is where I stood.
Everyone was giggling, this was certainly the day from hell,
it's so unfair, why me? It wasn't my fault I fell.
After assembly had finished and everyone left the hall,
Headmaster asked me if I'd learnt my lesson by standing up the wall?
I said yes I have but I don't know if I should say,
but when tomorrow morning comes, in bed is where I'll stay!

Nicola Pitchers

MY STROKE

At 6am I lay in my bed, a terrific pain came into my head.
An Aspirin tablet I did take, to see if I could quell the ache.
The tablet did not do the trick, I now began to feel quite sick,
I think to the hospital it's got to be, let's see what they have
                                                    to say at A&E.
I was admitted, they had a plan. After tests, I'd have a scan.
The scan results will take some time, we'll draw some fluid
                                                    from the spine.
The net result was not so good, the spinal fluid was full of blood.

I lay there upon the bed, my arm and leg were going dead.
To another hospital, we must transfer, you will have an
                                                    angiogram whilst there.
The angiogram showed quite a lot, I'd had a stroke caused by a clot.
This was the time to cast a tear, part through worry, part through fear.
I pondered and thought throughout the night, this is going
                                                    to be an almighty fight.
I've got to make this feel like fun, learning again to walk and run.

The OTs came to help me dress, my first attempt was quite a mess.
A finger flickered and then a thumb, this was when the fight began.
The physio showed me what to do, how to walk I hadn't a clue.
But listen, learn and persevere, and always have your brain in gear.
To the doctors, nurses, physios and OTs that through their
                                                    dedication and expertise . . .
I can now walk, pull, push and say, thank you!

Ivor Emlyn Percival

A Poem Dedicated To The West Pier

I stand alone in the ocean, cold and rough
 The serenity never reaches the English Channel

I'm old and tired
 But not under the shadow of Brighton Pier

I shine only in the evening.

Yoshihiro Okumura

PAINTED LIFE

I want to paint my life,
the way it's always been
I want to paint all my treasures
and things that I have seen.

I'd like to paint the smell of spring,
or the crunch of autumn leaves,
the crackle of ice underfoot,
or days of summer breeze.

I'd like to paint these ever-changing moments,
those rare and special times,
to paint them in colours bold and bright,
- this is the life that's mine.

I'd like to paint my life - in a future far from now,
and hope that through all those changes,
my paint stays bright somehow.

L O'Rourke

ENGLISH BREAKFAST

It said: £6.25 for an English breakfast

I said: £6.25 for an English breakfast?

She said: £6.25 for an English breakfast,
    Now how would you like your eggs?

I replied: Faberge . . .

Jon Oyster

Pride

A huge big truck
Watched through a leafy arch
Behind the wheel he sat
Tooting the horn, 'I'm home, I'm home.'

In front of the TV
He'd sleep for an hour
Resting his eyes
While waiting for dinner.

Bunnet and jacket then went on
'Takin' the dug a walk, Nan'
Round the village he'd go
Stopping to gossip
When pals were met.

November we always watched him cry
One weekend in the year he remembered
All who left but never came home
A blood-red poppy he wore with pride.

To me a gift he gave
He showed me what true sacrifice is
So now I too wear my poppy with pride
As a mark of respect to him and his friends
Who in whatever way fought so true and brave.

Agnes Neeson

THE BLACKSMITH

Frosted windows share their light
The solitary moon hangs high and bright
Fire the forge another day
Fill the net with sweet mown hay.

Stray cat and kits are doing fine
Makes this her home from time to time
She stays until her young are grown
Then find herself another home.

The postman calls, he's nearly home
A stocky man chilled to the bone
We talk and pass the time of day
Then with a smile he's on his way.

A wagon and team on passing through
The leading mare has thrown a shoe
She's quiet, she's a gentle soul
If served she'll throw a handsome foal

It's midday says the old church clock
I finish the school house broken lock
The builder's boy who is running late
Wants hinges for a kissing gate.

The parson calls late afternoon
He brings with him the squire's groom
The carriage has a broken wheel
And his cook provides an evening meal.

Now it's late, for all is dark
I make my way across the park
The cold cuts through me like a knife,
But I know she waits, my dear, sweet wife.

K S Nunn

A POEM

A poem is like sweet fragrance of burning incense
that can turn your spirit intense.

A poem touches your heart,
like incomprehensible abstract art.

Unpredictable like straw under the summer sun,
a poem stretches from a rhyme to a pun.

A poem is like molten rock,
it can take many shapes and forms.
Now a simile then a metaphor.

Like quick silver on top of waves,
poems can be onomatopoetic raves.

A poem can be harsh or euphonic,
it can teach knowledge or tell a story.

A poem can be put into a song
and be played all day long.

A poem can fall at the bottom of your soul,
settling like snow without making any noise at all.

A poem can space inside yourself
as long as your imagination . . .
will never end.

Giovanni Nacci

LITTLE WILLIES

Our life jackets were not enough
As the Lord's water became more tough.
Within that swirling, sizzling sea
It tisn't the place to be.

Tisn't the place to be.

A Norton

ONLY FOOLS AND PANTOUMS

The Trotter boys lived down at Peckham,
In a tall high-rise block council flat,
Things constantly threatened to wreck 'em,
Del's business sense took care of that.

In a tall high-rise block council flat,
They felt fortune would one day be theirs,
Del's business sense took care of that,
They both wished to be millionaires.

They felt fortune would one day be theirs,
Selling hooky gear, they ducked and dived,
They both wished to be millionaires,
So towards that end, they both connived.

Selling hooky gear, they ducked and dived,
Hoping things would get better one day,
So towards that end, they both connived,
Waiting for good luck to come their way.

Hoping things would get better one day,
'Stead of giving each venture their best,
Waiting for good luck to come their way,
It's the wrong recipe for success.

'Stead of giving each venture their best,
They sat around waiting for luck,
It's the wrong recipe for success,
They continued to dive and to duck.

They sat around waiting for luck,
So all that they tried turned to dust,
They continued to dive and to duck,
In ability, they put no trust.

So all that they did turned to dust,
The Trotter boys lived down in Peckham,
In ability, they put no trust,
Things constantly threatened to wreck 'em.

Mick Nash

GRAVEYARD

Love lies dying
in the graveyard of my heart,
and all the warmth that I once felt
has started to depart.
Now the coldness is creeping in
to freeze love where it lies,
and I'll place a stone above its head
when it gives up the ghost and dies.
I have no thought of rescue.
I won't save it from its fate.
My heart is all but frozen
and now it's just too late.
I want love to be gone from here
and never see its face again.
And I won't mourn for the loss
of that which brought me pain.
But maybe I'll visit the grave
to give myself a reminder,
that living without love
is lonely but much kinder.
And if somehow it's resurrected
to haunt me through my days,
I'll just drag it back to the graveyard,
for that's where my heart stays.

M M Graham

AN ODE TO THE QUEEN OF THE STREET

I picked up my Mail and shouted oh no,
The most famous landlady is leaving the show.
Three nights a week Bet brightens the screen,
She's got warmth, humour and wit, and is many a man's dream.
She was an instant hit when she walked in the Rover's door,
With her hair piled high and earrings that touch the floor.
She can move you to tears clutching a double gin,
With her boobs popping out in her dress of leopard skin.
But if anyone crosses her she'll just give a glare,
If the part calls for no make-up, she'll leave her face bare.
She's had many lovers, who have all been and gone,
And a one night stand with one-legged Don.
Hollywood can keep their stars, the Redfords, Newmans and Gere
But you and the Street beat the lot, and we just want you here.
So Bet please don't go, say it isn't the end,
For me and millions of others, it'll be like losing a friend.

Eileen Glenn

DECAY

All is still, in expectation
Of a new day, born free and clean
And the world awaits with trepidation
As warring countries fight for what has been
Freedom is no longer sanity
As peoples exploit the evil mind
Of the dictators' despotic vanity
That threatens all mankind

In life, in sport, at work or play
As the hours labour on
Evil means abuse the day
Before the sun has shone
No peace worldwide for us
As the tyrant welds his sword
And ashes turn to dust
A dying world is left to decay.

Margaret Gurney

A River Through Time

Life seems to be
Like a river through time
It runs ever onward
No reason or rhyme
Flowing so quickly
The hours into days
Months and years then
Disappear in a haze
The dear childhood memories
The learning and growing
Adventures and dreams
Ever onward then knowing
Far in the distance
We face the unknown
Like a river through time
There are blessings untold.

Jeanette Gaffney

WWW.WHEN WILL WE SEE, SET EVERYONE FREE.UK

When will all the hurting cease
so all the world can live in peace?
Who can rid the world of evil greed
and give the people what they need?
Why does so much go to so few
what on earth can we all do?
All of the world's governments, how, where or when
will begin, to put the world, together again?
When will they find war is no solution?
It only adds to the global pollution.
If the world can be allowed to sow and to reap
and all of the commandments we are to keep
open your eyes, look at the global scene
it's cratered with war, not lushful and green.
Children should be happy, playing, having fun
but before they can walk they learn of the gun.
Hatred and fear, hurt, war, or starvation
it's ravenging this world, it's in every nation.
No one is safe, each country is at war
for it's not safe on the streets anymore.
Money is the king, greed is the lord
people want what they cannot afford.
It's, 'I want this, I want that, give it to me now!'
If they can't have it, it turns to a row
some cannot have, so it's drugs or it's booze
it's a slow, lonely road, where we only lose.
Evil is winning, it's eating life away,
killing with greed, each and every day.
Splitting up families, killing each other
every mother and father, neighbour and brother.
When will the hate, hurt, evil all cease
when can we all, learn to live in peace?

Carl S Fricker

BEWITCHING WOMAN

Criss-crossed patterns off ridges and waves,
Besets to highlight the persona I seek and crave,
Her russet to strawberry blonde - crimped hair.
Causing me into a mystical place - to stare.
And it's touch 'are so subtle - does me enslave,
With its belied softness like velvet or sumptuous fur.

Underlined with bewitching eyes of emerald green,
Captivating and hypnotic always - whenever seen,
Whose lustrous gaze is so sincere - yet bold.
Placing my over zealous emotions on hold.
Desiring to claim these cherished jewels - to glean,
Total possession of me by them, as permanently sold.

And those sensuous lips embellished glossy red,
Fill lonely nights without you in perpetual dread,
So soft to touch - passion consuming with desire.
While yet always setting my besotted heart on fire.
To be once more engulfed by them - paradox swayed,
Adrift in ecstasy transported to paradise or higher.

All before is further enhanced - combined together,
Where no artist could improve - create better,
In the permutation of your elegantly defined face.
As to this embodiment of bewitching sublime grace.
Causing my enraptured soul to be stole into fetter,
Yours always to control as motivation becomes displaced.

Gary J Finlay

THE VOICE

When all around had disappeared
One remained by choice
Though timid, much is surely feared
Expression is through voice

Such mighty force from one so shy
An angel lays the note
Amid the sound; a passer-by
Forgets a winter coat

Hidden well, he dares to near
The beauty that is reached
And thus, the only one to hear
The music he has preached

He listens to this girl defeat
But utters no remark
With revelled smile, he leaves the seat
And fades into the dark.

Kerry Feild

CHILDREN

Their voices carry as if to say
I really enjoy coming out to play
TV is for those who cannot go out
Or for those who just want to hang about.

For games outside are so much fun
Even better when we can see the sun
For those days that are, now long and bright
As we stay and play until it is night.

And before we are finished at the end of the day
We will make plans for tomorrow as we say
We'll meet sometime after ten
And start our games all over again.

Now they are older, so what do you think
Some are now tied to the kitchen sink
While others at college, or got a good job
Trying to impress and earn a few bob.

And so as the days get cold and grey
Those mates we all knew some gone away
To other countries, or to the grave
And the rest left with memories, just to save.

The childhood of old that we once knew
And where we always found some things to do
With no evil thoughts to fill our mind
Not like modern kids of a different kind.

Imelda Fitzsimons

THROUGH THE WINDOW

Through the window
Seen the light of day
As dive the swallow
At their play
The sun glistening
As though jewels surround
Giving a heartfelt feeling
As thou look around

Through the window
Beauty can be seen
As far as the eye can follow
Filling one with esteem
So magical the scenery seems
One feels in a far off land
Such is sweet dreams
Brain filled with plan

Time ne'er stands still
As the sun slips away
Thy heart in thrill
Thou emerge through the day
With renewed power
And feelings of ecstasy
Thy heart feeling lighter
The day ending in a gentle breeze.

Josephine Foreman

ELEVENTH

A brief September, early morn
Come, had been a lifetime's scorn.
Jackers hi had bade their time
Need not of a call remind
Those innocent people caught in flight
Were soon to feel the jackers' might
They'd planned it all from years gone by
To terrorise, destroy imply
As was their cry, 'What so my life
Who cares of others or that man's wife?
We are but chosen for this act
Will see Creator, a common fact
Bound in sunshine far away
Our lifetime wish is here today.'
God so would turn within His grave
To see such evil and hate be gave
This, not of His mind
But peace on Earth
Do live as one, fulfil my birth.
But jackers are crazed and torn
And have in mind this early morn
To commit you all onboard to death
This plane will crash with every breath
Say your prayers, your time has come.

Hugh Campbell

BLACK WIDOW

Her life has gone sour
She rents rooms by the hour
Her life has reached a very low ebb

But she does not care
For she's laid in snare
He'll be caught in the black widow's web

The life of the spider
When there's no one beside her
Is lonely, and no one will care

They used her, abused her
Tricked and confused her
The spider goes back to her lair

Another day dawns
And she starts to stare
She gets out of bed
And brushes her hair

She puts on her make up
So they will not see
The tears she's been crying
Endlessly, endlessly

The telephone rings
And she answers the call
A customer speaks,
'Is she dark, is she tall'

The man disappears
After leaving his gift
But this is small comfort
For it will not lift
Her spirits, they're ebbing
When will they flow?
When will she know
True love?

S Farley

A TEDDY BEAR'S PICNIC?

To stand in front of a redwood tree,
Is, to experience, the power of nature.
Overawed, you feel - humbled, exhilarated,
Yet privileged, to see such stature!
Imagine then, as with outstretched arms,
You attempt, to encircle a tree,
Backs, to its trunk, two of you stand,
For photographs for posterity,
When turning to see that you are at the end,
You are face to face - with - a bear!
Who had wandered, out of the forest,
To see what you are doing there!
Quickly but silently, edging away,
Eyes averted from that Bruno's stare,
You stumble backwards, to reach your car,
So thankful, you left it just there!
When you get home, your photo reveals
What a lucky escape, you'd had!
Tho' who surprised who? was the question!
That bear, really didn't look bad!
Would he really, have used those claws?
Were those teeth bared in a smile?
We were intruders, in his domain,
Who had lingered for too long a while!
I guess the moral to this little tale,
Is to keep your eyes open, for bears.
Especially when on the redwood trail,
And remember that world is theirs!

E M Eagle

SEVENTY

I had my 70th birthday (just the other day).
I seem much older than when I was 69.
My brain has shrivelled.
I lost the way
When I parked my car. Which is mine?

I had a red one last week, maybe it is green.
I tried the lock. It didn't fit.
These vehicles were much too clean.
The key slid into the blue one. This was it.

I had driven to the shops at the double,
Though I'd left my list on kitchen table
I didn't let that cause me trouble.
I was sure it was quite memorable.

Now where did I put that shopping?
Oh! There it is on the back seat.
To go back again would be shocking
I think I remembered all I need to eat.

Three times I fumbled in my pockets - no key.
I searched through the shopping bags - not a trace.
Then I saw that key tucked away in my tree.
I must have put it in the usual hiding place.

I opened the door. It was good to be home.
I sat down and made myself a cup of tea.
I dozed by the fire I had no more to roam.
Then remembered the petrol gauge showed empty.

I should have to walk uphill to the village -
Three miles there and three miles back
For an old lady this is quite a mileage.
Was the can in the greenhouse by my anorak?

Jane England

THE SEED OF THE SOUL

Inside every conker there a seed be
Which with nourishment becomes a tree
People too have seeds inside
Inside a dark, social shell it has to hide

Before, your seed was afraid to sprout
For fear others would scream and shout
Keeping up your false facade
Holding your beautiful, unseen potential barred

Don't wait until the autumn of your life
Before confronting this self imposed strife

Reach for the sky, reclaim your star goal
Perform the work that is in your soul
Let the sun's loving light shine on your inner seed
And live the life nature intended you lead

Painfully splitting apart your spiky shell
Developed through years of conditioned hell
Is a long and painful journey
But leads to who you were always meant to be

A beautiful tree.

Andrea Darling

YOUR OCEAN LOVE

My love is on a never-ending tide,
It reaches you and dances with your pride.

Your ocean weeps, its every drop a tear,
You meet me, greet me and then you disappear.

Wild horses on the surf keep us apart,
Waves roll me onto stones that cut my heart.

Your sorrow pulls me to your heavy pain,
You take, let go and push me back again.

Your ocean weeps, its every drop a tear,
You meet me, greet me and then you disappear.

Carol Ann Darling

My Worst Nightmare

Walking home on a dark winter's night,
After alighting from a crowded bus.
Heavy footsteps I heard behind me thus,
The street lamp flickers out - no light.

The footsteps get closer and faster,
My heart starts pounding so loud.
I start running with head bowed,
Alas fear has become my master.

Should I knock on a stranger's door?
To ask for help and shelter.
What am I waiting for?
My mind's like a helter-skelter.
I know I can't run anymore,
My legs begin to falter.

I tell myself to behave normally,
To pretend everything is fine.
The stalker catches up with me,
I feel like I'm treading a fine line.
Time assumes a dream-like quality,
As I face the stranger with calm resign.

Rosemary Davies

NOTHING LEARNED

I've been down roads that had no answers
I've walked through flames that didn't burn,
I've fallen ill, but cured no cancers
I leave this place with nothing learned.

I've felt the pain without the suffering
I've lived the storm without the rain,
I've spoken clearly through my stuttering
I leave this place feeling the same.

I've broken my wings, yet still I fly
I've been cut deeply with no scars to show,
I've sat in the dark with the morning sky,
I leave this place as cold as snow.

I've seen others in pain, and felt no sympathy,
I've received presents, and given no gifts,
I've solved many mysteries in life so easily,
I leave this place without having lived.

Paul David Dawson

THE MAGIC OF BADBURY RINGS

I know a delightful place you may like to go
It is an earthy Badbury Rings
Where wind strongly blows!
With the hills slow falling down on the Dorset sky
Close by, an avenue of 365 tall trees
All in an unwaving line.
As the picturesque road drops down then raises gently up high
And gladly the sun may able to brighten up
And shine on your day
As shadows can form into golden rays of sunlight
While on the worn out stoney by-ways
The horses footprints turn right
And left or out of sight,
The serenity is always there
For you to ramble or to ride
Whilst all the animals are free to roam with nature's pride.

Sammy Michael Davis

DEAR MUM

It was the sort of day to give ten out of ten
I wouldn't do now, but I didn't know then.
The sky was blue, the sun shone proud
Wild flowers and butterflies, I sang out loud.
You did not mind when I walked alone
I wasn't that far, I could see my home.
You warned me of strangers, and not to talk
Take sweets, a life, or go for a walk.
I'll try to explain why I never returned that day
So dry your eyes and hear what I say.
I'm there when you cry, I'm there when you grieve
I love you Mum, and I'll never leave.
I walked to the edge, it was calm and still
It beckoned, I dived, it gave me a thrill.
I swam and splashed, and had such fun
The water cooled me from the blazing sun.
I was then taken under, caught in a tangle
The sun above the water, a giant gold spangle.
I wanted you Mum, I tried to shout
I was filling with water, I couldn't get out.
I kicked and fought, the weeds held strong
It was over Mum, I didn't suffer long.
So murky and dark, the taste of the mud
That's what took your flesh and blood.

Stephen Denning

STILL

What do you see when you look at me?
The happy young girl I used to be
Or the ageing body no longer free
To jump and run and dance with glee?
And do you love me still?

What are you thinking when you stare
At my now lined face and whitening hair?
Are your thoughts of memories that we share
Of love and closeness today so rare?
And do you love me still?

What do you feel when you meet my eyes
And take my hand and don't disguise,
A blaze of emotion, contented sighs
A warmth projected from eyes so wise?
Yes you love me still.

W A Ronayne

INSPIRATION

Where is the muse, to make my pen fly free
Or the imagination to capture what I see?
The images to stipple my blank page,
The visions to show that I am sage,
The boats to float on metaphoric sea.

I seek to find a most profound message,
Who will set me free from my word-blind cage?
I try and try but the words just flee,
Where is the muse?

Who will loose me from my misery?
I do not know, where or what I be.
I'd like to take my place upon the stage
To pour forth some of my verbal rage.
I cannot find my way to liberty,
Where is the muse?

Frank Keetley

TONGUE-TIED

I see him walking down the street,
And know that we're about to meet,
I feel my heart just skip a beat!

He smiles at me as he draws near,
My heart beats fast, with love? Or fear?
I just can't speak, so shed a tear.

He hesitates, then walks on by,
If only I were not so shy!
But if he said 'Hello' - I'd die!

I'm sure that given half a chance,
We could have a big romance,
I pause and o're my shoulder glance;

Just as he looks back at me,
I wonder can this really be?
He smiles and waves - I laugh with glee!

I feel a blush suffice my cheek,
The wave returned, my knees grow weak,
Next time we meet I'm sure we'll speak!

Ailsa Keen

I KNOW YOU KNOW

Mixed up all the colours, stirred and blended themes,
Put the spark into the void and electrified the schemes,
Brought life to thoughts I had dreamt of long ago,
Forcing me with their laughter to find out what I know,
Can I really work it are the words good enough,
Haven't got what it takes to wing it on a bluff,
For every word written; a visual can be seen,
Always be somebody else that stands where I have been,
As island in the ocean; a fight beyond the bell,
I know they are nodding; I know they know too well.

Karla Kerr

LABYRINTH OF LIFE

This picture is life's moral maze
From which there is escape
A labyrinth that you can get through
To give your life new shape.

When in the depths of deep despair
A tiny glow of light
Will guide you through the barriers
And help you make things right.

Take the path that leads you
To a bright new day
Opening doors to wonderment
Again - it leads the way.

For the flickering light will brighten
And the darkness fall behind
All barriers will diminish
As you break the chains that bind.

Until, at last, you make it through
The web of discontent
Surrounded by the light of life
To a future of intent.

Sandra Kinnear

TIDY

Tidy thoughts show a tidy mind
Free from stress to unwind
A tidy look and tidy hair
To show the media that you care.

Search for something you cannot find
Brings to thoughts, a tidy mind
Among the many places to look
For that particular, letter or book.

To enter into a beautiful house
All credit to the owner's spouse
Who has a careful tidy mind
Not knowing what visitors may find.

Looking on at passers by
An odd assortment, you will find
Untidy hair, and nondescript dress
Crumpled trousers, and short skirts no less.

There is a place for everything
And everything in its place
Results of untidiness there's no trace
But a tidy mind with care and grace.

So bare in mind a tidy thought
And be grateful you were taught
Then you will find an easy mind
Remembering chaos and leave it behind.

C King

WITHOUT YOU

Build me a boat
Strong and true
Where will I go?
I'll sail to you.

Knit me a coat
Thick and warm
To warn off the chill
When you're not home.

Buy me a dog
Loyal and kind
To accompany me
When you leave me behind.

Build me a house
Cosy and small
A place to dwell
Till I hear your call.

Grow me some food
To keep hunger at bay
For me to cook
When you are away.

Donna Kane

STICKY BUN (BRIMHAM ROCKS, NEAR RIPLEY, YORKS)

I'm a shadow of my former self
As you can clearly see.
I sit up here on Brimham Rocks
Enjoying my sticky tea.

This bun will always keep me fed
In weather cold or hot,
For here I am for evermore
In stone on this outcrop.

So - what made this all happen here
You may be asking now.
I'll tell you - it was very strange
But here's the story how . . .

My friends all thought they'd play a joke
Crept up behind - said *Boo!*
They frightened me to death and now
I'm turned to stone - it's true!

But I've the last laugh to be sure,
Instead of one short stay
I'll look upon the length and breadth
Of Yorkshire's pride each day.

This glorious countryside is mine,
Into my heart it stole
And in the core of this cold stone
Is buried deep my soul.

Paddy Jupp

INSOMNIA

Sometimes when I go to bed,
I can doze until noon,
Other times when I go to bed
I wake up all too soon.

There are times I know I'm tired
But cannot get to sleep,
I have even tried the old remedy
Of counting bloody sheep.

I'll toss and turn, shuffle about
Throw back the nice duvet,
I'll fluff up all three pillows
It's no good either way.

I've tested cocoa and Horlicks
Even a night-cap or two,
Nothing seems to damn well work
What else can I do?

Don't want to use sleeping pills
As you can become addicted,
Just want a good night's snooze
Before the night's evicted.

I'll maybe catch an hour or two
It's not quite the same,
As having those eight long hours
The Sandman is to blame.

I've tried every cure for insomnia
But nothing works for me,
I'm fated to lie awake for ever
As you can plainly see.

I'm sick of this sleeplessness
It's keeping me awake,
I think I'll make a cup of char
And watch the dawn break.

George S Johnstone

AS I LOOK

As I look through the window I see,
Such pretty things looking at me.
They have a lovely straight figure,
I hope they grow much bigger.
The garden looks so green 'n' lush,
Spring's come early, little buds on the bush.
The skies have cleared, the sun has shone,
Wet, cloudy days, I hope have long gone.
Easter is late this year,
I must ready my garden, then sit with a beer.
I must go to the church service today
Jesus has risen the service will say.
My wife with her Easter bonnet, will enjoy her stay.
As I look out my garden again,
A cloud looks, 'Oh go away rain.'
Those pretty things seem to look 'n' smile
'It's OK the sun will shine for a while.'
How beautiful they look with their golden glow,
My lovely daffs in a cluster they grow.

Carol John

MOUSEY THANKS

My best friend
    had a mouse,
On her landing
    every night,
So she left him,
    a nice piece of cheese,
and thought he'd
    be alright,
But he got so fat,
    and couldn't get back,
So 'disappeared',
    and so,
He left a note,
    to say,
'See you soon,
    thank you kindly
I've got to go'.

E B Holcombe

What Makes Me Smile

The sun peeping through black clouds,
A robin begging on my window sill,
Seeing the first daisy at springtime,
These all make me smile.

A cuckoo announcing spring's arrived,
The bleating of the newborn lambs,
Watching them frolic around the farm,
This makes me smile.

A bouquet of bluebells brought by a child,
The sound of laughter at your surprise,
The silly questions they often ask,
These all make me smile.

I smile at fond friends lost,
And the new friends I have made,
I smile a lot, nearly all the time,
It brightens up my day.

Jane Margaret Issac

MEMORIES

Happy memories of a time so true
All the trust I placed in you
But underneath you didn't care
Instead you dropped a bomb and left me there.

All the times I defended you
Yet in reality, I didn't have a clue
There was no truth; just hurt and lies
Now it comes as no surprise.

Those years they meant the world to me
But I guess it was never meant to be
After all the things you've put me through
I know there's a better person inside of you!

Maria Jenkinson

PUNISHED WITH PRIDE
(Dedicated to Faye Marsden)

Your pride is a crutch,
it haunts you so much

like a psychological warfare game
slowly it's driving you insane

I was your moral warrior
who stood by your side.

Your true feelings I never declined
held your hand whenever you cried

I never pushed your pain aside

I made a true love stance
you never gave us a chance

now your pain is engraved upon my face
you feel no shame and call it - grace

until the final day our true love died
all for the sake of your foolish pride

and from that you can never hide.

Graham Hare

ALTER THE CLOCKS

Alter the clocks! The nights grow chill.
Harvesting's done, though apples still
Cling to the boughs where tinted leaf
Not long defies that stealthy thief,
The frost that comes to cleanse or kill.

Will birds and beasts men's law fulfil?
Should they, like us, obey its will?
Absurd indeed were such belief
    In altered clocks!

Frost rims the pane with sculptured skill,
Ice gathers on the window sill.
Fast pass the days with joy or grief,
Nor can our faith or unbelief
Nor any deeds our hearts may thrill
    Alter time's clocks.

Kathleen M Hatton

SYMPATHY

I know your wife has left you
So you need sympathy
But there's no need to worry
She's come to live with me.

Austin Healey

FRIENDS

A friend is someone who is always there,
Whose friendship is constant with no ties to bear,
In laughter and tears or when troubles are near,
With kindness and caring over the years.

When a shoulder is needed our friend is on hand,
Giving time to reflect, not time to pretend,
We count our blessings that we have friends,
Who'll be there with us right to the end.

We exchange ideas and holiday stories,
We take advice or discuss our worries,
But in the end we're there for each other,
The blessing of friendship, the being together.

Elizabeth Hiddleston

DAYLIGHT

Daylight breaks the boundaries of the night,
Waves crackle against the shore,
The clifftops erode from their glorious height,
Wind hurries forward in an almighty roar.

The sun peaks from behind the seaside,
Blinks and lets an enormous yawn,
Water ripples along the bank, here comes the tide,
Fish swim wild and free as if they've been reborn.

Whispers of the world lapse over the land,
Seagulls smiling with warmth at the music being made,
Wading in and out of the sea and falling on the sand,
Happiness all around until the sun starts to fade.

Kimberly Harries

EMPTY

I sit here on my own and my mind travels to the past
I can't think about the future because everything's moving too fast
I think of my life as I slowly grew up
But it all seems so pointless as I stare into my empty cup
I feel loneliness is everywhere that I go
It's like I'm always knocking on an empty door
It feels like I'm locked in some big empty room
And every wall I turn to is filled with gloom
Everywhere I look darkness is what I see
Do you feel the same or is it just me?
Why am I doomed with emptiness all my life?
Don't you think I've had enough trouble and strife?
I feel like this from dusk till dawn
Is there any reason for my life to go on?
Why am I here? Why am I living?
It's not for the take; it's not for the giving
I've travelled this road looking for the light
But sadness and loneliness is all that's in sight
Show me the way, please show me the way
Show me to happiness where I can stay
Take me away from my life that's so blue
Please won't you say I can stay here with you.

Karl A Hunter

WHAT DO YOU SEE?

She sits rocking in her chair, staring into space
supporting her arched back is a cushion of lace.
I see the telltale life lines on the wrinkled frail skin
What is she thinking? What stories lie within?

She entered this world greeted by others
Four older sisters and five noisy brothers
Money so scarce, food hard to get
Jobs hard to find, living in debt.

Smoky days, so cold, so long
But she remembers her family so strong
Long working hours, then chores at home
Cooking and scrubbing, never being alone.

She remembers her teens, reflecting back on life
A smile at remembering becoming a wife
Then three babies which soon grew and left
Then illness came and put her man to the test.

Now, loneliness all around her, her husband long dead
She has all those memories (which are seldom said)
Her body now crumbled but her dignity she keeps
Upon life's reflection she silently weeps.

She moves her head and looks with those tired eyes
It was then I was able to realise
'Look at me,' she said, 'Look closer and see,'
Not at this old carcass, look closer at me.

Do not ignore me, I'm still on this Earth
I've ninety years of living since my mother gave birth
So talk to me, ask me, look deeper you fool
I am a living person . . . it's just life that is cruel!

Jo Hodson

ATTITUDE CHANGES

You never really liked me, I could tell all in your stance
Even when we were thrown together at the school dance
Don't they make a lovely couple I often heard folk say
You hated this when all was revealed and me with dismay
In class you were obliged to sit with me, I detested this every bit
Ignoring you continually, as with the others you made a hit
Silly girls would flock around you and make me feel embarrassed
You were their idol as the class now is on an educational trip to Paris.

I will not be going as my parents are not able to afford the fare
All the class are chattering and I am made aware
You, yes you are standing and with me wish to remain
The class and teacher are horrified what was there to gain?
The class depart and we two are assimilated with so many others
He is now very attentive and concerned like a brother
My parents say he is a nice boy perhaps my views will change
Though he still does a lot to annoy, and I readily fly into a rage.

I am told this is the process of growing up, and still he taunts me
Tolerating his behaviour he is still a child playfully
The class return from Paris France, and tell us what we missed
He ignores their foolish prattle and rewards me with a kiss
As teenagers we now step out as together we do not hide
He tells me one fine day as he loves me that I will be his bride
A honeymoon in gay Paris as we paved these scenes along
He and I must graduate which cannot be that wrong.

R D Hiscoke

ON THE THEFT OF A FRIEND

In the dust of this last extinction,
I am powerless to act,
In the fall from grace
Of another face
Of distinction,
It's a fact
That truth cannot exist here,
For expulsion from the hive will occur,
And those of us who survive, concur,
Lay service, with our lips, to the queen,
Share our honey, unseen,
And as the house, of cards, tips up slowly around us,
The candle will light us to bed,
While the chopper is waiting, poised
To play nursery rhymes
With our heads.

Susan Harwood

THE GAINSBOROUGH LINE

I use these words to paint a scene
Of leafy lanes and willows green
And viaduct across the Colne
Dwarfing Chappel - quite alone.

Next village halt - so very small
From Bures Mount the gradients fall
To tumble into valley steep
Reedy Stour at peace - asleep.

Thus terminus in Sudbury Town
The sprinter train - all creamy brown
Brightens up a morning grey
Skirting Cornard to Marks Tey.

Steve Glason

Early, Early Musicals

Warner Brothers, brothers they
Found a wonder, wonder way
To blow away, away the gloom.
Blow the horn, blow the blues,
To blow you out, to the moon.
Certainly without a doubt
Keeping all depression out.
Busby Berkley came to fame,
Musicals made his name.
Long legged ladies
All in a row, kicking high,
See them go.
Bring the Gold Gold Diggers on
Magic motion picture's fun.
Tip, tip, tappa tap
Dancing feet
Into Forty Second Street.
Synchronised moving fine
Perfect precision,
Of a chorus line
A glamorous, glittering centipede
Like a, like a, kaleidoscope
Changing, changing at a stroke
First a girl, then a bloke.
Lights and cameras,
The opening bars.
Here comes the movie stars.

Glorious on the moving staircase
With beaming smile,
Max Factored face,
Ageless pictures that are now
Still alive, showing how
Flights of fancy on parade,
That's how musicals were made.
Yahhh!

Brian Benjamin

IS THIS THE ANSWER TO A PRAYER?

I got on a bus in Kidsgrove
The noise from two parents and a child was loud and raucous.

I turned around and caught the youngest's eye
I pointed to him and then did say:

'Diddle, diddle dumplin, my son John
Went to bed with his trousers on,
One shoe off and one shoe on,
Diddle, diddle dumplin, my son John.'

The silence was cutting
Then smiles and relief followed.

As I left the bus the driver thanked me!
I too was pleased and so were other people!

Marie Barker

BUNNY RABBIT'S SEEDS OF LIFE

Bunny the rabbit has lots of seeds to sow,
Nice green cabbages he hopes to grow.
For the best seeds bring the best crop,
To put a spring in any bunny's hop.
And by the harvest of his seeds,
Bunny the rabbit can meet all of his needs;
But Bunny the rabbit has a lot more seeds.
To plant all along the way,
We are all farmers at the end of the day.
You see, Bunny the rabbit knows,
That everything starts with a seed and grows.
Not just seeds that you put in the ground,
But seeds of love, goodwill and friendship found.
Much happiness and joy does the seed of life bring,
When the harvest of your seed begins to spring.
But remember, the best seed brings the best crop,
So start planting those seeds and do not stop.
There is one thing that will make your heart sing,
It is when the seeds of your harvest begin to spring.

Linda M Breeze-Gray

CHANGES

What changes to us does life bring?
Some that makes the heart sing
Some that makes the heart weep
Our souls to sigh and ever keep.

What change you ask affects us most?
Is it change at work, a change of post?
Or change of matters most financial?
Or other changes circumstancial?

We move our home - a changed location
A brand new job - a fresh vocation
We meet new people - how exciting
Now the future looks inviting.

The change of life - the menopause
Another change - but here I pause
To ponder deeply - reflect a while
On other things - that bring a smile.

The joy of birth, who can resist
A newborn babe - oh! utter bliss,
What pure delight in such sweet innocence
Of God's creation - of such magnificence.

Our lives speed on - our childhood flees
Away on wings of zephyr breeze
Our children grow and leave our nest
To roam the world - it's for the best.

With every change, there is a loss
And then a gain - the coin does toss
And flip and spin, then falls once more
Another change lies on the floor.

So, why does change feel so like fear?
To some, not others, year by year
But then we know at the final curtain
Change is the only thing that's certain.

If we nod to change - do not resist
Or struggle or fight - we're often kissed
By the breath of spirit - which softly blows
Into our heart - a peaceful repose.

Gina Bowman

THE DISTANCE

Where are you, Child?
    Where have you gone?
Your mother waits here for so long.
Have you drowned upon the seas,
Or lost your way amongst the trees?
Been buried with your memories?

Oh, mother's love,
    Why can't you know
Of all the ways I miss you so?
My journey ends before it starts,
Yet every night you're in my heart,
How cruel our lives wrench us apart.

Where are you, Child?
    Where can you be?
My love, have you forgotten me?
Has passion clouded so your thought?
Your lifetime lost in wars you fought?
Forgotten all that you've been taught?

Oh, Mother, dear,
    What can I say?
I am so very far away.
Such distance further than your call,
Beyond the ivyed garden wall,
Too frail now, to return at all.

J A Brown

PICKLE
(Sonnet on the death of an astronomer's cat)

Last night I saw a new star in the sky,
By name Felix Feles, a happy cat,
With noble head held high and proud, and that
Great glorious banner tail erect and high.
From those green eyes, like shining moons, that catch
Reflected light from every twinkling star
He sees across the universe afar
The great cat Leo, keeping kindred watch.
Only an amber shadow haunts my home,
And silence reigns where rolled his rumbling purr.
I miss the silken comfort of his fur,
The garden's empty where he used to roam.
In life he gave us all unstinting love,
Our heartfelt memories now are all we have.

Eileen Burgess

THE CASTLE

It stands so grim on yonder hill
A lonely castle, silent, still
And if those walls could speak - who knows
What tales of glory, grief and woes
What tales of laughter, joy and tears
Would fall upon our listening ears
T'was built in days so long ago
A fortress built against the foe
It's massive walls are crumbling now
No voices speak to tell us how
They lived and died here long ago.

For who can tell and who may know
Who fought and won, who fought and died
How they rejoiced or why they cried
A sentinel it stands there still
In ruins now on yonder hill
For everyone who laboured there
Have gone - no more of grief and care
For they have gone as go we must
Reduced like all things into dust
It's mute no message can it send
Before it too - to dust descends.

Lydia Barnett

THE FIRST BLINK

The clock began to tick five thousand years ago,
In Sumer, a society we might know.
Until our sun burns out? Five *billion* more to go.

If we imagine our tenancy of Earth might last
For just one day, only a fraction of a second has passed.
In that short blink, we've travelled far and fast;

Shakespeare, Mozart, Christ have come and gone.
We have the wheel, electric light, medicine, have bounced upon
The moon. And yes, I know, there's also the atomic bomb,

And some still think talk's worthless, prefer to fight.
This race knows how to kill itself - and might.
But I like to think there is a distant, flickering light

Along our evolutionary tunnel. Less than a second's gone.
Hold on. Have hope. The whole day's yet to run.

John Andrews

OLD AGE

Life is very cruel as old age devours the body,
The walking is more difficult, and the breathing very dodgy,
I used to think nothing of walking mile after mile,
But now old age has got me, a yard takes a while.

What happens to the body when old age gets to grips?
Looking in the mirror at the thinning of the lips,
Lines across the forehead which when young were completely sealed,
Old age has dug more deeply now, they look like a ploughed field.

The teeth look really good they are white and trouble free,
This is easy to explain, they don't belong to me,
The hearing is getting worse, and I really need an aid,
So I have decided to get one made,
The choice was quite prolific, so I went and chose the best,
Now I wear it all the time, thanks to the NHS.

The neck is getting scraggy as the skin begins to crease,
When will this devouring ever, ever cease?
The chest hair is now grey, where once it was so black,
And the skin around my breasts is hanging like a sack,
The swelling of the stomach, is where the chest has dropped,
And going further down, you would think I've had the chop!

Why oh why I ask, will this devouring ever stop?
This is only one answer
When they screw down the top.

Thomas Ainsworth

FOR AMY

It was ten years ago when I died of the flu,
I'd had a good run . . . well I was eighty two!
My friends were so sad when they heard I was ill,
My family anxious to be in the will.

Those posturing vultures wishing me dead,
As I choked and gasped to demise in my bed.
Then the lawyer read out my final intent:
That all of my relatives get not one cent,
Except for granddaughter Amy McCoy,
Should inherit my wealth on the birth of a boy.

This money in turn should be kept in trust,
To bring him up properly, honest and just
At age twenty one it would pass down the line,
To increase on the wealth as though it were mine.

Now I lie in the womb awaiting rebirth,
In a couple of months, I'll be back here on Earth.
Then I'll gurgle and giggle and splutter with joy,
As I gaze up at Mother . . . my Amy McCoy.

Andrew V Ascoli

LONGING

The days merge into nights
Dull, dark and oppressive.
Bitter winds scald hands and faces,
How are we equipped to forgive?
Momma dear I cried last week,
In my mind's eye we speak
Of trivial things, shopping and food
Sad thoughts, I choose not to brood.
Tears flow freely to mark your death,
I was not there to feel your last breath.
So much to say, so much left unsaid
I can only rehearse words now you are dead.
Anniversaries are kept in my heart
Pictures soothe my soul, for my part.

What did my counsellor say:
Your mother would be proud.

Sarah Allison

UNTITLED

Sunday travellers
The meek and the mild
Those that seek
Those that hide
The strong and the rich
The wrong and the poor
Those who belong to the pitch
Those who belong to the tour.

Philip Allen

NO OIL PAINTING

If he never had any hair
Would they vote for Tony Blair -
Lived next door at your neighbour
Would you go out and vote Labour -
Wore silly clothes like Mr Ben,
Would he get in at number ten,
If he was to act all sinister
Would he have ever been Prime Minister.

If he had hair in an Elvis quiff
Would people vote for Duncan Smith,
Or had some old foolish superstition,
Would I still be there in opposition,
Made a scandal that set out a story
Would more folk admit to being Tory,
Joined the BBC as a news reader
Could I become a real party leader.

Or is it down to these names
Everything would still be the same,
If as a great lover I was hot
Would it help elect John Prescot?
Or was less of a bore
Could we have a Lord Jack Straw?
Is it fate that God did bring
For looks are not everything.

Colin Allsop

WINNER TAKES ALL

A little slow, not too bright,
Always seemed to be in a fight,
Other kids laughed at you,
You had some friends, but only a few,
How you hated going to school,
As the other kids thought you were a fool,
It seemed as though you couldn't win it's true,
But your parents had great faith in you.

You were a kind and sensitive child,
Although when you were cross you could be quite wild,
So your dad took you to the local gym,
And an old pro boxer let you spar with him,
You were good he told other folk,
Suddenly you weren't such a joke.

You are on telly tonight,
In your first professional fight,
Out you come, strutting your stuff,
And you certainly look mean and tough,
You found what you were good at, and showed the world son,
Tonight was the first of many such nights
And best of all, you won.

Maureen Arnold

SWING LOW

Roy Hoskins was buried today,
The poor man had such a hard life.
He coped very well in his way,
Despite all the struggle and strife.

Everybody said they loved Roy,
Yet it didn't do him any good.
The community gave him little joy
And didn't care as much as it should.

So starvation then was his end,
To think too, in this day and age.
Perhaps a message it will send,
And evoke all of our rage.

Where were we when Roy was in need,
His suffering was apparent?
Not even enough for him to feed,
Shame for a man of such talent.

So to Roy, I say goodbye,
In heaven I'm sure you'll play guitar.
Such a disgraceful way to die,
I know you could have gone so far.

To myself and to society,
I say hey! Stop and have a think!
How low our sense of propriety,
Are we all prepared to let sink?

Arthur

IT TAKES TWO

They often make promises they don't intend to keep.
Want to share your bed at night - but snores disturb one's sleep.
They'll walk the dog; they'll feed the cat.
But turn a deaf ear when you chat!

They'll disappear behind the paper oblivious to all.
Keep the TV sport switched on when friends decide to call.
Disaster falls; they're never to blame
Admit they're guilty? Shame oh shame!

On the other hand, they're useful going off to shop.
Help with the credit card should your balance drop.
We'll put up with their quirks and turn a blind eye.
Men are from Mars! Change them? Don't try.

Women are creatures of many moods; they often have the blues
Cope and manage, do not complain, or be idle, if they choose.
Budget carefully, then off on a spree,
'Buy that new dress? Oh no, it's not me.'

His parents visit at Christmas; she'll cook a fantastic meal.
Eat and drink, enjoy the day - then say how fat she feels!
Look after the family - act as chauffeur
Plus washing and polishing - cleaning the car.

She'll fiddle and natter, filling her time,
Until cooking the dinner, three courses and wine.
Out with her friends to a show or a movie,
This girl she's from Venus - she's cool and she's groovy.

Pamela Carder

THE SAILOR

Her heart stood still as she suddenly observed him,
Sailing slowly, and with carefree ease upon the blue and white boat.
All at once he drew nearer and waved, almost as if in recognition,
A passing stranger, who brought a tear to her eye and a
                              lump to her throat.

For a split second she had thought him to be someone else,
A man of the salt and sea, who still ruled her heart and mind.
She was transported back in time to a long lost paradise,
Where two lovers had sat and watched the sunset, their arms entwined.

How easily she recalled the warmth of the fading summer sun,
Whose rays had highlighted stolen days, filled with
                              passion and heartache.
They had both longed to reside in their own secret cocoon forever,
A fantasy dream world, from which neither ever wanted to wake.

Eventually the sun had set upon them for the final time,
As fate intervened and decided that they were not meant to be.
And today as the waves lapped softly and gently around her,
She recalled how they had sailed a far more turbulent sea.

Memories tossed and turned over in the midst of her thoughts,
As she watched the yacht caress the smooth ocean waves.
All too soon it merged with the horizon line and faded in the distance,
Like her former existence, now a long ago, faraway haze.

The wind propelled her vessel forward, and he was finally
                              lost to her line of vision,
As she journeyed upon this new voyage across the bay.
She now knew how fortunate she was, to take a part of her love
                                           with her,
Into a different time, a different place, a brand new day.

Mary Carroll

THE COAL PLACE

The coal place was filled up for winter,
Two hundred pounds it cost us all in all,
I look and say - are you worth it?
I shouldn't grumble - you will keep me warm.

Every morning, noon and night,
I empty ash pan and fill bucket
Some drops onto the path, I have to pick
It up, you are a nuisance,
Damn the stuff.

Back inside I stack you on the fire,
Don't put too much on or it will go out
'Let it breathe.' Says the man about the house.

Twice a week I wash the stove down
If I want hot water, I stoke up in the night,
When I came from work last night,
You'd burned away,
The place was freezing cold.

I slip about the snow as I pile you into the bucket,
The ash blows back into my face,
Damn the stuff,
Why can't I burn gas?

Janet Cavill

YOU AND ME

Today, this person is no fool
It's ages since he attended school
He can do things, which others cannot do
Leaves people thinking, and you know who
His brain can still remember, lots of things
Like helping others, and the pleasure it brings
Then all of a sudden, it all comes to an end
Nothing, just nothing, just waiting for it to mend
So, remember the days of long ago, everything so free
Loyalty, how costly it turned out to be
Now sit down, switch off the TV
All this applies, to just you and me.

Walter John Coleman

TILL DEATH DO US PART

Shadows thrown across a room
Signify your time of doom
Welcome forth or welcome not
Fit the shape into the slot.

Metal object raised to strike,
Sharper than the sharpest spike
The red curtain will soon be drawn
And another life embarked upon.

Soul flying to the sky -
End of life, time to die
Invitation not yet sent
Time to send the sacrament.

N Barry-Mills

My Mum

Spring 1987

My mum is someone you could not believe
Beyond the realms that minds conceive
She's really very scatty headed
With a view like a church with windows leaded

She tries so hard to do good deeds
But no one cares or no one heeds
She joins in most the things she can
But what she needs is a real nice man

Someone who could care for her
Keep her all wrapped up in fur
Be tender, kind and loving too
Oh what the hell are we to do?

She puts men off right at the start
She's lost that loving, wooing art
How will she ever turn them on?
If she doesn't hurry they'll all be gone

Oh come on Mum, do your best
Flutter your lashes; leave off your vest
Make the men sit up and stare
Or soon there won't be any there.

10th October 2002

So she fluttered her lashes and did her best
And picked out Eric from all of the rest

He took her to places that she'd never dreamt
In return, she gave love, and showed him what it meant
They got on so well in work, rest and play
That they became even closer day after day

She touched all those she met with her vitality for life
Cared about others, was a mother and wife
Her innocent outlook on things that she saw
Made her endearing and left us wanting more

But now you have left us, what will we do?
We'll miss our best friend, cos Mum, that was you.

Jill Corkish

ENCORE

Oh no! I've got them again!
As soon as they leave their bed
The music is pounding in my ears.
All I can see is red!
My wonderful neighbours have gone,
The ones I have now aren't the same.
They couldn't care less about others
I might not even be 'in the frame'.
If I try to watch television,
And I do keep the volume down,
They're sure to like different stations;
For noise I'll give them the crown.
I thought it was too good to last.
Wherever I've lived before,
I've only had peace for a short time
Then noise has been the encore!
I wish I could put them in orbit
Way out on a journey to Mars . . .
Send them all in a permanent circle
Along with their boring popstars.

E Balmain

ABUSER

He's evil and slimy, well men like that are,
They take no prisoners and leave deepest scars,
They work undercover and find weakest prey,
They chip off their armour and eat them away.

The slow unseen slices of family and friends,
Will vanish so slowly and hold no end,
The woman will lose all she once held so dear,
And many a moment will spill into tears.

She gives him her heart, but he won't stop just there
He takes all her mind, all her values and care,
Imprisons the soul and corrupts the mind,
Makes seeing the person she was hard to find,
Then there's the child, my granddaughter you see,
Being given to him like his property.
A small innocent voice who's his victim it's true
Then he tries to destroy her world as she knew.

I'll still be there for her, no time can erase,
The feelings and bond that I carry no haste,
No haste and no hurry, I'll sit back and wait,
For the time that I'm needed, oh God keep her safe!
I try to think logic and calm and pure thoughts,
It's really hard not to hate him and his sort.

What makes them like it? What makes them maine?
Like sons of Satan again and again,
But little one's angels will guard her I know,
My prayers may be answered and one day he'll do,
He'll crawl on his belly and find weaker prey
And carry on eroding all pure love away.

Diane Blount

A WEEK OF MEN

I loved Tom truly on a Monday
Thought he was a good-for-fun day,
It turned out that I wasn't right,
He stole my purse and left one night.

I loved Malcolm on a Tuesday
Believed he was my real-good-news day,
How could I have been so wrong?
He was married all along.

I loved Simon on a Wednesday
For him I gave up meeting-friends day,
Yet again I was mistaken,
My credit card was used when taken.

I loved Colin on a Thursday
Thought it would be give-me-furs day.
Oh my dears, was I in error,
Mean as Scrooge and what a terror!

I loved Stephen on a Friday,
Dreamed at last that this was my day.
All hopes were dashed once more of course,
He stole my car to buy a horse.

I loved Peter on a Saturday,
Here for good the one-that-mattered day.
Another time that I was conned,
He dumped me for a dumb young blonde.

I met no one on a Sunday
And had a jolly chap-free fun day.
Made a future solemn vow,
No more, no men, no love, no how!

Sarah Blackmore

LARK ASCENDING

Full throated to the universe
Lark ascending spills its verse.
To hen that closely mothers chicks,
In that tussock that she picks.

To greater heights with lilting trill,
As with air its lungs does fill.
It tells a story to the world,
With that crest so lightly curled.

This bond, a very gift of nature,
In meadows may no longer feature.
But mountain tops are their domain,
Since farming is now so profane!

Telling stories of summer hay,
Where its chicks were wont to play,
This is a gift of country riches,
Surely it each one of us bewitches?

G Buckland-Evers

JUST A DREAM

A dream of dreams my golden dream, only a place
where my dream and I have been,
Share this dream with me; don't stay behind, for it is a dream
so wonderful and yet so kind.
Take one step forward and gently hold my hand for this is the
beginning of my dream to a wonderful land.
Gently close your eyes and slowly count to five, now we can meet
inside my dream staring at glorious and wonderful golden blue skies.
Travel with me now on this journey to a land of my dreams so far away,
and forget all those troubles that you leave behind,
for they can wait for tomorrow day.
Feel yourself lift now so gently high up into the sky,
for you now travel with me in my dream through those
golden blue skies.
There will be no rain clouds allowed into this wonderful dream of mine,
Just choruses of dancing music which sound so wonderful and sublime.
Look down now and you will see the snow white ripples
of a great and beautiful calming blue sea, and there just in the
distance I can see the island of my golden dreams that waits
for you and me.
Walk with me now on this island of my dreams with its golden
soil so precious so warm,
Fill the clean air you breathe is it not as pure as the
first day you were born,
We could both stay here for evermore in this wonderful dream
of mine, or shall we both return home when tomorrow comes,
and tell others about this dream and where it began from.

Alan Brunwin

How We Love To Queue

Standing in the longest queue,
Just two girls on the till,
You only want to buy one item,
The crush and squeeze starts to tighten,
Her in front with full trolley,
Pays by cheque, she has no lolly,
The one behind, in your back,
Just knocked over the offer stack,
Correct money in your hand,
You wonder, how much more to stand?
It's now my turn, it's looking sweet,
But now she's out of till receipt.
'I'm sorry luv won't be a mo,'
Do I stay or do I go?
You work out what you will say,
Now you've waited half a day,
You're burning now, to insult,
Then decide, it ain't her fault.

A A Brown

THANK YOU FOR MY GRANDSONS

Thank you God, for Kieran
He is my first grandchild
So thoughtful and so caring
He can always make me smile.

Thank you God, for Shaun
The second to come into my life
So laid back and full of humour
Shauns' planet, looks just about right.

Thank you God, for Adam
He is the third to come along
Such a contented and happy baby
My feelings for him are just as strong.

When I look at my three boys
I think I am well truly blessed
Made them all their own little people
And let me have the very best.

So as I lay down to sleep
God can you hear my prayer,
Look after my three little boys
Because I know you always, will be there.

Margaret M Donnelly

HOLIDAY TAN BLUES

Bright orange orb in the sky
Makes me want to close my eyes
Burning rays shining down
Makes my nose look like a clown
Should I use cream or a lotion
Wish there was a magic potion
Lying here is too slow
To give my body a healthy glow
Oh boy I need a drink
Still no sigh of turning pink
Off to the bar for some shade
Have a drink not lemonade
End of the day what a fright
A bright red nose and a body of white
Same routine every day
And still looking very grey
Returning home on the flight
The odd one out
The one that's white.

J Alan Crook

ELSEWHERE

Sorrow makes us refugees
who crave this Elsewhere land - its ease,
its greenest grass and cloudless skies,
where tears are dried from brightening eyes.

Anger makes us call for maps
to guide us there, to show where traps
may lurk, to lure us from the way -
the pilgrimage - to endless day.

Terror makes us doubt we'll find
this golden land. We look behind
and all is dark; we look around -
nor life nor light can here be found.

Then joy arrives and, by its light,
we know no cause or need for flight:
Elsewhere and Here are but one place,
so lift to Love your trusting face.

Lucy Crispin

RISING UP

Ups and downs	up
Standing	Rising
Falling	up
Down	Climbing
Feeling	up
Down	Standing
Fallen	up
Grace	Coming
Fallen	up
Disgrace	Waking
Broken	up
Down	Fixing

Wendy Chaffer

WE PLAY OUR PART

Everybody has their dreams,
Of things they wish to do,
But we must also play our part,
If our dreams are to come true.

If it is a material dream,
Saving is a must,
If we do not do this,
Our dreams remain as dust.

If we could save some money,
Put a little away each week,
It would then become reality,
No longer a dream we speak.

Let me give you an example,
I hope to make it plain,
Two people with the same dream,
Their circumstances, the same.

Who do you think will win their dream,
The one who squanders away,
Or the one who puts a little by
And gets nearer to the day?

The daydreams become reality,
For the squanderer it will never be,
As he has wasted all he had,
His dream he'll never see.

The one who put a little by,
His dream he did gain,
And forward he then will go,
Another dream to attain.

The squanderer has little,
Not much has he to show,
Yet he says of the other,
'The lucky so and so.'

Luck had nothing to do with it,
'Twas just a dream at the start,
But dreams become reality,
If we do play our part.

C S Cyster

ANOTHER YEAR GONE

Another year gone.
Another war won.
Another war going on.
Another life lost.
Another homeless one.
Another lonely one.
Another battered one.
Another loved one gone.
Another hungry one.
Another poor one.
Another suffering one.
Another broken heart.
Another broken life.

C J Walls

THE BEST CHRISTMAS PRESENT EVER

I caught an image at the glance of an eye
Something so amazing was passing by
Accompanied by a jolly laugh were a few words spoken
'My reindeer broke down,' he said, just joking.
Turning my head to see an unbelievable sight
Eight tiny reindeer carefully landing from flight.

I rubbed my eyes, because I thought I was deceived
Looking at something I would have never believed.
The snow fell silently as it covered the ground
The jingle of bells was the only sound.

As I ran outside onto the garden path
Once again I heard that jolly laugh.
It made me smile and feel like a child again
When I used to imagine my Santa Claus friend.

I folded my arms to try keep me warm
It was so cold outside in this wintry storm.
He looked at me as he got in his sleigh
A wink and a wave, then they flew away.

Running back inside thoughts flew around my head
This image I'd seen from the window by my bed
Turned out to be something I'd stopped believing in
But this little appearance had made me believe again.

Zoë Thompson

NOT GENTLE, JUST SCREAMING

A senior citizen!
I never intended to be.
I don't know how it happened
It just crept up on me.
A committee lady? - Yes
in glasses and a hat.
A playwright or a poet -
how ridiculous is that?

I might be one of those
who goes *completely* off the rails,
shouting, 'Free condoms for pensioners,'
or, 'Give the vote to snails.'
I might take up pole dancing
or join a belly dancing class.
I might chase every man I see
and even make a pass.

I'll grass skirt in Hawaii,
Go nude in St Tropez,
Get arrested in Montmartre,
but *I'll* sing another day.
I can see it all quite clearly,
my past has been *too* tame,
but I know just who the culprit is,
my *youth* deserves the blame.

Helen R Eccles

GRANDAD, MY BEST FRIEND

My grandad, he made baskets for Pearson's Pottery;
Not the kind for shopping, but for the King's navy,
To hold mercury by the gallon and the sailors' rum,
That needed fingers strong and sure, with a tight and steady thumb!
The willows came from King's Lynn, not split but whole and brown
That, soaked in an iron bath outside, its icy waters caused a frown!

I would call at dinner time, on my way from school,
And he would show me caps he'd made on a little stool.
He showed me how to try my hand to pull the willows through
But, though I tried so very hard, that I could not do!
Grandad's hands were soft, though strong, from witch hazel in the cane
And, despite the willows' icy wetness, no chapping did sustain.

Saturdays I'd shop for him, with his basket round and deep
Filled with groceries to the brim, to climb the road so steep!
I started that at seven years and earned a threepenny bit,
But all that fresh air and exercise I reckon kept us fit!
And afterwards he'd entertain with sayings and a trick
For, tho' turned seventy, he'd still cock a leg o'er walking stick!

Grandad and I were good pals and on Sundays went for walks
Across the fields and through the woods - how I enjoyed our talks,
The many laughs together and calls at farms and cotts,
Where I would sing for friends and of cakes and sweets, get lots!
I'd get a silver sixpence and milk straight from the cow,
Then meet our friendly cousins, and watch the farmers plough.

Grandad had funny sayings that caused us both to laugh,
But Mother got quite angry and told him not to be so daft!
He'd tell me tales of yesteryear and we would laugh some more,
And I was Oh so happy, it didn't matter we were poor.
For bonds of love 'tween young and old, that spend their time together,
Ne'er dull, even when the old are gone, but thro' the years
                                                           will weather!

Bee Wickens

WISE PARENTING

Teach your child and tend the vine
Fill with love this soul divine,
Water it daily, its branches prune,
Each single birth is Heaven's boon,
Show you care and set the scene
While the tender buds are green.
Give it values to live by,
Share together, laugh and cry.
Heart to heart communicate,
Form the bond before it's late,
Speak of spirit, a model be,
Spur it to its destiny.
At times warm, but sometimes firm,
Be the harbour in the storm,
In daily prayer put your trust,
Spirit feeding is a must.

If your training is done right
You will lead that child to light,
Prompt the vision, a noble cause,
Teach it to obey God's laws,
Then as your old age sets in
You'll be blessed and both will win.

Emmanuel Petrakis

OUR LODGER

Our 14-year-old grandson, Chris, asked one day,
'Nan, Grandad, can I stay?
There's no room at home, well none that you can mention,
It's just until we build our new extension.'

A teenager to care for after all these years,
'I'll be fine' he says, trying to allay our fears.
So in he moved, baggage and all,
His pin-up posters on his bedroom wall.
His music, games and mobile phone,
Now he really feels at home.

The months pass by, extension plans are slow,
But Chris seems in no hurry to go.
He's pretty good though and rarely seen,
But when we get home we know he's been.
With his bedroom we do despair,
His school clothes scattered everywhere.
The phone bill's doubled, there's washing aplenty,
He's raided the fridge, it's almost empty.

His 15th and 16th birthdays go past,
Extension plans are passed at last.
'Not long now' we say, three is a crowd,
But when he left school we felt so proud,
In his suit and bow tie and standing so tall,
He looked real cool, going to the school ball.

He wasted no time, he didn't shirk,
He wanted to earn, he wanted to work.
On his 17th birthday I had a bouquet,
Chris said, 'Nan, I go home today.'
As I wiped a tear, he gave me a peck,
He said, 'I'll be round' but has he heck!

Cynthia Pitch

COMPANY

I am a peaceful lady
Who enjoys good company
Being serious all the time
Certainly isn't me.

I have a happy-go-lucky nature
And I love to have a laugh.
Guess I am like a bird
To be tied down, I can't,
I have to feel free.

Never can I explain myself,
Though I know what I mean.
Sometimes what I say
Makes others cross with me.

Seeing folk with gloomy faces,
Makes me feel so sad.
'Smile Dear,' I want to say,
'You'll see things aren't all bad!'

Doreen Petherick Cox

I Wonder Why

I wonder why the grass is green,
I wonder why the sky is blue,
I wonder why the sun is yellow,
I wonder things about you.

I wonder why your nose is long,
I wonder why your eyes are round,
I wonder how you run so fast
Around the playground.

I wonder why we're called humans,
What does it really mean?
I wonder why a book's a book
And why a bean's a bean.

I wonder why we are what we are,
Not somebody else or thing,
I wonder why it's cold in winter,
And why flowers grow in spring.

Bethan Gifford (10)

WHAT'S THE WORD I'M LOOKING FOR?
(For Gemma)

Words hanging off a picket line
Shouting to be heard
Like a tabloid's headline, on the table
Digested with breakfast, how absurd!

The words profoundly travel light,
Stepping into our intellectual skin
Mixed with cornflakes, milk and sugar
Like a verb without a sin.

They store away in tiny cabinets
Files so thick, yet bare
Cobwebs keep them company
Forgotten in myths who they forbear.

But I knew some of these words
Like friends we used to share
We danced upon space and time
We did each other's hair.

But not all words are gracious
They sometimes bite my tongue
It's these careless, spiteful demons
That make you want to curse.

Like little soldiers with their hats on
Some straight, some round, some tall
Made up of many syllables
Imprinted onto walls.

With these little words I live
In calm and stormy seas
On occasion we battle till the dawns of time
At dusk we sing under the trees.

But all really I want to know
Is where these words are now?
I read them just tomorrow
Today they left me with no vowel.

J L Copestake

SAVE ME (COS I LOVE YOU)

Come and save me, my friend in spirit,
I spoke to you during my stay,
Although you didn't know about it.

You were all that kept me going, my pal,
While away I had many a conversation with you,
Though I doubt whether you really knew.

Your wistful solipsism and bittersweet humour,
Saved me from a brain tumour.
The image of you in your cool NHS specs,
Took me to Fantasy Island,
As my mind started to flex.

I'll love you as a brother,
And though you've been proverbially banned from our home,
I'll look up to you like no other.

You've got to let me know where you are.
Free me from the knot they've tied,
Or my stormy brain could soon get fried.

The image of you, Gladioli in hand,
Helped lift me away from this stinking land.
They're trying to drown me under white-hot spouts,
These knots are the same bloody ones
They teach you in the scouts.

Simon Cardy

HUMILITY

To grow and show all that you know
To live and let your heart's love flow
You must come back to the place called home.

If you stray too far, when you turn to see
The place you call home, is nothing but trees.

Like the great lessons in life
To be humble is to love
To respect is to make it known
That you come from a place called home.

Everyone comes from a place called home
A place where love plays like a musical tone
Where love has no masks but filled with the past
So to be humble is to love,
The place you called home.

If you are humble then you'll know the way home
Where the welcome is fit for a king on a throne.

If you stray too far, then you'll never see,
The place you called home is nothing but peace.

When you turn around to go back to peace,
Then all you'll see is nothing but trees.

Dennis Lye

A NEW KIND OF WARFARE

A new kind of warfare:
Where all weapons fired
Return to their senders,
In great curving arcs.

That combines the best
Intentions of the suicide bomber . . .
With the friendliest of fires -
And no collateral damage whatsoever.

Peter Asher

EASTERTIDE

Springtime wipes away the winter gloom with April's tears
Daffodil, crocus and snowdrop now appears
Life begins again to thrive in tree and hedge and field
As gloom and frost and darkness remember they must yield
To summer's distant challenge that sounds in treetops tall
From every waking creature and every song bird's call
It's a time of new beginnings and hope comes in its train
For Easter is upon us and the world is young again
And as our world wakes up again and nature's cycle starts
May springtime warm our very souls deep within our hearts.

V J Askew

CAPTIVE

As our eyes met, I knew I'd found my destiny.
From the moment you smiled it was so meant to be.
And now when I think of you I feel that same thrill,
A feeling of happiness and elation lingers there still.

The thrill of your gentle touch, or a lingering kiss.
When we are apart it is you that I miss.
Since meeting you my life has been fulfilled.
On a foundation of love each day we build.

We build strength, we build trust, trust in one another;
Every day of our lives, new discoveries to uncover.
Reaching onwards towards the same shared goal;
We are true soulmates in mind, body and soul.

Maggy Copeland

A SIMPLE LIFE . . .

A simple life, no tangled web
No jewels or riches, no fame or celeb.

A pleasure to visit, in window a wave
To all who crossed threshold, such pleasure you gave.

No large house or manse, but room in your heart
To keep others dear, even if they're apart.

Your passing leaves sadness, an empty, dull pain
And all that is left are the flowers we have lain.

But there's more when reflecting on memories stored
Sammy, Major and Ben - dogs you adored.

The garden you sat in, feeding birds from above
Your flowers all thriving from gold touch and love.

Puzzle books near the sweet tin - on settee you curled
Not much on TV! All trouble in world!

Feelings are strange on the M25
Remembering visits when you were alive.

Now Earth's door is closed, new window you'll view
While we journey forward, remembering you.

So thank you, God bless you, over years you'd become
Much more than an in-law . . . *my surrogate mum.*

Di Castle

WHEN GOD MADE TIME . . .

They say when God made time that He made sure
we'd all have quite sufficient, but I find
that more and more it seems there's less and less
to do the things to which I am inclined.

I'd love to spend more time in quietude
deliberating all things heavenly;
to probe the puzzles of the universe
and float away on clouds of fantasy.

To be at one with ev'ry living thing,
to be afraid of no one nor despise
the right of anything that lives and breathes
to share all that exists beneath God's skies.

To feel the heartbeat of the living earth
when life is somewhat dull and meaningless,
and through life's bedlam feel its rhythmic pulse
and find myself some kind of peacefulness.

To be assured that someone has prepared
a destiny for ev'ry single soul,
and though at times it seems all is not well
to know a greater force is in control.

To feel that presence always by my side,
to feel secure, protected from all ill;
to feel His strength, His arms encircling me,
completely acquiescent to His will.

So if, when God made time He made enough
for us to do the things we have to do,
and if we're all a part of His great plan,
why is it that, for me, it isn't true?

Hilary J Cairns

DROP OF PLEASURE
(Xmas 2002)

We sail a rolling ship,
Each day we do the same trip,
From bed to toast, and sweetish tea,
For ever the same trip, for my mate and me,
Sailed to new port for Xmas Day,
Just a stop to pick up some store,
We have done this many times before.
Build my own boat,
Wanting just compass and map,
Then up with the sail,
Can't say when we'll come back.
Today is different,
A boat comes to our port,
'Twill tie up and drop anchor,
Short stay, the permit's clear.
Then up with the anchor,
Sailing back to home port.
For a little while, we shall alter our style,
Not so quiet, a change of diet.
For a while,
The quiet days will be,
Silence will come with its pots of tea,
Relax to what we had,
Just Enid and me.

Harold Cotterill

THINK OF HIM

See that man stumble, crippled and old.
One day his story, his life will be told.
No one asks him about things he has seen.
He tells no one about the places he has been.

See in his eyes the pain that's lingering there.
He lives his life but with no one to care.
A lonely old man with his stories to tell.
So who really cared when this old man fell?

Believe me or not, that man was a hero
In a war long ago, medals of valour not on show.
This living hero saw many of his friends die.
Distant memories now, in his dreams he cries.

A crippled hero, as he moves painfully along.
Remembering happier days, those happy songs.
Leaving mates behind, buried in some foreign soil.
Now each day is painful, doing his daily toil.

Think of him as you slowly pass him by.
He fought for you under dark grey skies.
Like many other heroes, they all went to war.
Many of his comrades, never to see any more.

Kevin P S Collins

HOSPITAL

Do not dread
being put to bed.
In the theatre
you may see pictures
even though you sleep so sound,
lions and tigers can abound.
You will wake up feeling sore
but there's a lovely meal in store.
Perhaps you'd like a nice hot drink?
That pretty freckled nurse, did she wink?

Cor! What a laugh
if she would help you with your bath.
You could undo the ribbon
which ties her lovely auburn hair
and watch it fall - just
as far as possible!

Now then, remember in the morning
to heed the surgeon's warning.
You . . . must . . . take it easy!

Kinsman Clive

ANCHOR BOOKS
SUBMISSIONS INVITED
SOMETHING FOR EVERYONE

ANCHOR BOOKS GEN - Any subject, light-hearted clean fun, nothing unprintable please.

THE OPPOSITE SEX - Have your say on the opposite gender. Do they drive you mad or can we co-exist in harmony?

THE NATURAL WORLD - Are we destroying the world around us? What should we do to preserve the beauty and the future of our planet - you decide!

All poems no longer than 30 lines.
Always welcome! No fee!
Plus cash prizes to be won!

Mark your envelope (eg *The Natural World*)
And send to:
Anchor Books
Remus House, Coltsfoot Drive
Peterborough, PE2 9JX

**OVER £10,000 IN POETRY PRIZES
TO BE WON!**

Send an SAE for details on our New Year 2003 competition!